WRITERS ON THE SPECTRUM

of related interest

So Odd a Mixture
Along the Autistic Spectrum in Pride and Prejudice
Phyllis Ferguson Bottomer
Forewords by Eileen Sutherland and Tony Attwood
ISBN 978 1 84310 499 5

The Genesis of Artistic Creativity
Asperger's Syndrome and the Arts
Michael Fitzgerald
ISBN 978 1 84310 334 9

The Girl Who Spoke with Pictures
Autism Through Art
Eileen Miller
Foreword by Robert Nickel MD
Illustrated by Kim Miller
ISBN 978 1 84310 889 4

The Myriad Gifts of Asperger's Syndrome
John M. Ortiz
ISBN 978 1 84310 883 2

An Exact Mind
An Artist with Asperger Syndrome
Peter Myers, with Simon Baron-Cohen and Sally Wheelwright
ISBN 978 1 84310 032 4

The Imprinted Brain
How Genes Set the Balance between Autism and Psychosis
Christopher Badcock
ISBN 978 1 84905 023 4

WRITERS ON THE SPECTRUM

How Autism and Asperger Syndrome have Influenced Literary Writing

Julie Brown

Jessica Kingsley Publishers
London and Philadelphia

First published in 2010
by Jessica Kingsley Publishers
116 Pentonville Road
London N1 9JB, UK
and
400 Market Street, Suite 400
Philadelphia, PA 19106, USA

www.jkp.com

Library of Congress Cataloging in Publication Data

Brown, Julie, 1961-

Writers on the spectrum : how autism and Asperger Syndrome have influenced literary writing / Julie Brown.

p. cm.

ISBN 978-1-84310-913-6 (alk. paper)

1. Autism in literature. 2. People with disabilities, Writings of, American--History and criticism. 3. People with disabilities, Writings of, English--History and criticism. 4. Authors with disabilities--Biography--History and criticism. I. Title.

PS153.P48B76 2009
820.9'3527--dc22

2009023999

British Library Cataloguing in Publication Data

A CIP catalogue record for this book is available from the British Library

ISBN 978 1 84310 913 6

Printed and bound by
Lightning Source

Contents

ACKNOWLEDGEMENTS 6

PREFACE 7

1. Introduction 13
2. Hans Christian Andersen 37
3. Henry David Thoreau 59
4. Herman Melville 81
5. Emily Dickinson 95
6. Lewis Carroll 117
7. William Butler Yeats 139
8. Sherwood Anderson 159
9. Opal Whiteley 181
10. Autistic Autobiography 203

FURTHER READING 231

Acknowledgements

Special thank you to Clatsop Community College, Astoria, Oregon, for supporting me while I developed the autism in literature class and did research for this project. Thank you to my smart and helpful student aids Jan Nerenberg, Eric Peterson, Jennifer Cerf, and Amber Caruthers. Claire Conklin and the CCC library staff helped me with inter-library loan, giving me access to the libraries of the world—I couldn't have finished this book without your help. Thank you to my kind editor Lily Morgan at JKP. Thank you to the Clyde, Ohio Historical Society, Public Library, and also these helpful women who enthusiastically shared their knowledge of Sherwood Anderson: Dorothy Cox, Brenda Stultz, Pat Gill, and Jill McCullough. Thank you to the University of Oregon Knight Library Special Collections staff for helping me learn more about Opal Whiteley. Thank you also to the staff of the Hans Christian Andersen Museum in Odense, Denmark for allowing me to use his manuscript and cutouts. A slightly different version of my Hans Christian Andersen essay first appeared in the *CEA Critic* (2008), helping me to get the word out about autism in literature. Thank you to my mother Renee Williams and my Uncle Gary Webb for your unwavering moral support. Thank you to my children Bobby and Maggie for putting up with me while I was so busy with this project—I love you with all my heart. I especially appreciate all of the conversations I've had with AS individuals through the Aspies for Freedom chat group on the internet—you guys are so amazing and your friendship has meant the world to me: Amy, Andrianna, Antiphase, Breeze, Cousin Luigi, Gwen, Lemonzest, Mayaku, Mel, Mich, Rosa, Serge, and Stuart. Most of all, thank you so much my beloved Zhaulds, to whom this book is dedicated.

Preface

Most people are not surprised any more when they hear about the relationship between autism and science or math. They are familiar with the popular images of the absent-minded professor, the mad scientist, or the mathematician who is more in love with equations than with people. Movies such as *A Beautiful Mind* and *Mozart and the Whale* have reinforced the idea that quirky, eccentric men can be extremely gifted with numbers. Many people can point to Albert Einstein or Bill Gates as individuals whose place on the autism spectrum gave them skills they needed to reach new breakthroughs in physics and technology.

People are less familiar with the idea that an autism spectrum disorder (ASD), including Asperger's Syndrome (AS), can affect those who work in the humanities and liberal arts as well. In 2004, Professor Michael Fitzgerald published his groundbreaking work *Autism and Creativity*, which analyzed connections between autism and the creative process. He argued that certain features of ASD, such as persistence, single-mindedness, intelligence, and non-conformity, can enhance not just the analytical process, but the creative process as well. He immediately followed up with *The Genesis of Autistic Creativity* (2005), which identified and diagnosed several writers, musicians, and artists whose neurological differences contributed to their unique ways of using language, sound, and color. Identifying talented individuals with autism in this way has been an important step in creating an awareness of "autistic culture."

Author Valerie Paradiž has also explored the concept of autistic culture, from a more personal perspective. While researching autism in order to better understand her son Elijah, she discovered that Einstein was considered to be autistic. This led her to explore the concept of an autistic social history, and she wondered, "Did Elijah possess a social history that he might call his own?" She continued to search for other historical figures that might have had autism, in order to learn about and embrace a heritage that her son could someday claim. She shares with us how "the very words 'autistic culture' had been humming in the back of my mind like a question mark ever since I had begun my research on Albert Einstein" (132). Her search for autistic culture fueled the writing of *Elijah's Cup*.

The research of Fitzgerald, Paradiž, and others has left me with lingering questions about how, exactly, ASD has influenced specific works of literature. Would *Alice in Wonderland* be different if Lewis Carroll hadn't been on the spectrum? Would a neurotypical Thoreau have written a novel instead of *Walden*? Why did Emily Dickinson use so many dashes? Was Hans Christian Andersen's *Snow Queen* somehow an allegory for autism? My musings led me to broader questions: Is there an autistic writing process? Do authors with autism have their own ways of using language? Do they develop plot, character, or setting in the same way? How does their narrative structure differ from that of neurotypical authors? Are they drawn to different topics or do they develop different themes? Other scholars have already identified and "diagnosed" writers who were likely to be on the autistic spectrum. That is not my project here. I am taking the next step—studying the impact that Asperger's Syndrome has on literary writing, and looking closely at how AS shapes the way that writers use the written word. Specifically, I am interested in analyzing the ways that Asperger's Syndrome influences writing process, form (structure, style, conventions), and content (character, theme, autobiographical elements).

Like many academic scholars, I was drawn to the study of Asperger's Syndrome because I have a child (born in 1994, the same year that Asperger's Syndrome was added to the Diagnostic and Statistical Manual of Mental Disorders—DSM-IV) who is on the spectrum. Learning about "what makes him tick and tock" (his phrase) has been a fascinating and necessary journey for me. My son's favorite subject is math (at 13 he was the youngest student enrolled in college calculus), but he is also a good writer—when he chooses to be. I noticed his flair for humorous writing early on. Some of his teachers have appreciated his penchant for slapstick, parody, and sarcasm; others have not. He nearly failed the seventh grade benchmark exam because, on a whim, he decided to write the entire essay examination in "hillbilly dialect." I thought it was well-written and hilarious. The exam committee did not. My research into AS and literature has not only given me tools to help me become a more understanding parent, but has also opened my eyes to a rich, beautiful sub-culture that I never knew existed.

As a lifelong writing instructor, I have taught thousands of students how to express themselves, communicate, and create works of art with their writing. In recent years it has been my privilege to work with college students who are on the autism spectrum. The college disability specialist understands my affection for students with Asperger's Syndrome and sends them all to my classes. Teaching them has given me the opportunity to observe closely the impact that neurological wiring has on how people write, what they choose to write about, and how they use language to represent themselves and their unique perception of the world. I enjoy working with this quirky, bright student population.

Finally, this book has been guided by my background and training in literary criticism. Ever since graduate school I have been drawn to authors who are not in the mainstream. We have much to learn by studying under-represented groups of writers to see how their writing both resembles and departs from majority culture. Previous projects of mine have included *American Women Short Story Writers* and *Ethnicity and the American Short Story* (both at Taylor and Francis Publishers). More recently, I have fallen hopelessly in love with the autistic literary authors examined here.

The process of selecting the 13 authors for this study involved reading biographies (several on each author, in order to gain a broader perspective), autobiographies (sometimes multiple versions), letters, diaries, histories, and literary works by a variety of authors—some well known, some obscure. Once I identified which authors I would consider, I pored over their poems and stories, their novels and plays, looking for similarities and trends within the group, pondering differences. Looking at hand-written manuscripts and rough drafts gave me insight into their writing processes. Re-reading journals and letters gave me information about their motives for writing as well as their attitudes about their finished works. Visiting the authors' hometowns enabled me to see a bit of their world. This research has been both thrilling and deeply satisfying for me.

For the past several years I have been teaching a special new course I designed called Autism in Literature, which focuses on books written by people on the spectrum: it is offered through the department of literature, not psychology, because the focus is on studying the literary merits of the chosen texts. Each term it draws a large number of students, including future teachers, future counselors, parents and grandparents of autistic individuals, and also students who are themselves on the spectrum. The course is valuable on so many levels: it gives neurotypical students a chance to understand and appreciate the contribution that individuals with autism have made to literature, while at the same time giving ASD students a chance to celebrate their own cultural heritage. The conversation and exchange of ideas between the students as we read through the literature together has been life-changing for many of us. It does make a difference, to many people, to know whether or not an author was on the autism spectrum.

Just as women, minorities, and gays/lesbians have made great strides in recent decades toward valorizing their achievements in literary history, so too should autistic/AS readers and writers claim their literary heritage not only for their own benefit but for the benefit of the neurotypical world as well. This study offers insight into how people with autism perceive the world and how they perceive themselves in the world—and how they translate that perception into a written text for purposes of self-expression, communication, and even healing. Language makes us human. By studying how writers on the spectrum use language to create art, we gain a wealth of knowledge about how the human mind converts thoughts and feelings into story, and converts story into abstract markings on a page.

It is my hope that this exploration and analysis of authors with autism will have a positive effect on the neurotypical world's understanding of autism. It is also my hope that this study will give ASD readers a chance to further explore authors who might share some of their life experiences, concerns, dreams, and struggles. It is my hope that for every time someone in the media mentions Einstein as an example of a person on the spectrum, he or she will be just as likely to mention Hans Christian Andersen, Lewis Carroll, Emily Dickinson, or any of the other writers included here. I want to celebrate the good news that many of the world's most important writers—those who have made original, brilliant, daring contributions to literary achievement—were able to do so, in part, because of their place on the autistic spectrum.

Works Cited

Brown, Julie, ed. *American Women Short Story Writers.* New York: Taylor and Francis, 2000.

---. *Ethnicity and the American Short Story.* New York: Taylor and Francis, 1997.

Fitzgerald, Michael. *Autism and Creativity.* New York: Brunner-Routledge, 2004.

---. *The Genesis of Autistic Creativity.* London: Jessica Kingsley Publishers, 2005.

Paradiž, Valerie. *Elijah's Cup.* New York: The Free Press, 2002.

CHAPTER ONE

Introduction

How Asperger's Syndrome Affects Writers

Autism is a unique developmental disorder that is characterized by impairments in social skills, communication, thinking patterns, and sensory issues. It presents itself as a spectrum, ranging from severe (the individual is withdrawn, non-communicative, seemingly unreachable) to very mild (the individual functions well in society but is considered to be eccentric or quirky). Asperger's Syndrome (AS) is a diagnosis given to certain individuals who are at the higher-functioning end of the spectrum who also exhibit high intelligence levels. No two people with Asperger's Syndrome experience it in the same way, but there are many traits that most of the individuals share in common. Since writing is a process that translates one's thoughts and feelings onto the page, the influence of AS on that process is undeniable, and expresses itself in similar ways from author to author. Some of the most prominent traits of Asperger's Syndrome are as follows:

- The individual struggles to understand social codes, consider other people's perspectives, and extrapolate motives—this can influence an author's perceptions of his reader and can also shape the way he or she develops characters.

- The individual's verbal communication is affected by a variety of problems—this influences the way an author uses language, impeding his ability to communicate to the reader but also paradoxically giving him or her remarkable artistic abilities at times.
- The individual has a rigid mindset and can lack flexibility in thought, behavior, or imagination. Such thinking patterns affect the author's writing process and many of the choices that he or she makes about genre selection and literary conventions. It also gives an author the ability to stay highly focused on a writing task for long periods of time.
- The individual often experiences a number of sensory problems or issues. Sensory perception can be acute, under-developed, lack integration, or be entwined (synesthesia). This contributes to the way an author translates the real, physical world into words on a page.

This book provides comparisons between several writers on the spectrum to see what kinds of commonalities we can find throughout their collective body of writing. These commonalities can then serve as indicators of how autism spectrum disorders (ASD) affect written communication. This book also seeks to isolate and study the individual differences that remind us that no two people are affected by autism in the same way.

1. A Messy Writing Process

Sifting through the manuscripts of the authors in this study, I was intrigued by how many brilliant writers, winners of world-wide acclaim including the Nobel Prize, had messy rough drafts. Their handwriting is often quite sloppy, in part, because of the *dyspraxia* (clumsiness) that many people with autism have. Thirteen-year-old AS author Luke Jackson commented on this challenge: "I do have problems with writing and that is a fine motor skill (though if you saw my writing you would not say it was fine). This just goes to show that when someone is interested in something, then it is much easier to overcome or find ways around their difficulties" (46). Remembering what writing a novel entailed before computers or even typewriters were around keeps us mindful of the Herculean challenge that writing an entire book posed for someone with clumsy, uncooperative fingers. As a result, the whole process of putting words onto paper often resulted in one big garbled mess. Hans Christian Andersen's friends often complained to him that his handwriting was hard to read. Black scratchy lines zigzag back and forth like lightning bolts across the rough drafts of his autobiographies. Thoreau's friends complained that they could barely read the letters that he sent them. Emily Dickinson's tiny poems were scratched out in handwriting that resembled bird tracks criss-crossing a snowy field.

Rough drafts often reveal an intense struggle with the process of putting thoughts onto paper that may also be due, in part, to the fact that many people with autism spectrum disorders are visual-spatial thinkers, while writing is an abstract, linear process. This creates certain challenges that neurotypical writers (who are more likely to be verbal thinkers) don't face. Temple Grandin reports that as a child she was subjected to a battery of tests that showed "even as a child, [I] scored at the top of the recorded norms in spatial tests and visual tests but did rather badly in abstract and sequential tasks" (Sacks 284). It's a bit like the problem of rendering our spherical Earth on a flat 2-D map—there is no easy way to do it, and certain distortions inevitably have to be accepted. Some writers with autism, including Sherwood Anderson, have solved this conundrum by writing with something resembling a "cubist" style of story. By assembling numerous small images of a story as viewed from various angles, something like the whole picture can be seen.

Many of the writers in this study used a *collage* process for assembling their drafts. Rather than sitting down to write a text from beginning to end, their drafts more typically had a hodgepodge look and feel to them, with bits and pieces taped or glued together to form a manuscript. When Lewis Carroll was a child, he edited a family newspaper, *The Rectory Magazine*, which consisted of little stories, sketches, and poems written by various family members (mostly him) pasted together in a scrapbook format. Hans Christian Andersen cut and pasted paragraphs from other texts, even those written by strangers, to glue into the rough draft of his autobiography. Opal Whiteley's entire diary was written on the backs of envelopes and old paper wrappings and was later torn into even smaller fragments—when she presented her manuscript to an editor in Boston, she brought him boxes of paper scraps ripped up into thousands of pieces and the two of them had to spend months piecing the journal together before it could be published. Emily Dickinson wrote her poems on pieces of paper she cut into small squares that she stitched together into little booklets she called "fascicles." This "bits and pieces" approach to writing is also no doubt fostered by the AS preoccupation with fragments (such as the way a child with autism might prefer playing with a toy wheel to the whole car).

Carroll's fascination with *collage* morphed into literary *assemblage* as he wrote *Alice in Wonderland* and *Through the Looking Glass.* These two novels were stuffed with quotations and allusions from dozens of other writers, as many as seven or eight per page. He wasn't the only one to rely heavily on literary allusion: William Butler Yeats was interested in Irish mythology and folklore, and many of his poems made a reference to something from the earlier days. James Joyce, who showed signs of AS, not only patterned his great novel *Ulysses* after Homer's *Odyssey*, but made so many literary allusions in the text that one has to search hard to find something that comes from Joyce himself.

The recurring practice of quoting from someone else's literature in your own text resembles the echolalia that people with autism are known for. Some repeat words from movies, television, or other people because they are trying to understand the meaning of the words. Sometimes echolalia is an attempt to communicate with others—the words are tools borrowed to build meaning. Some repeat phrases for the sheer joy of it. Several of the authors with autism studied here who add esoteric quotations from classical Greek texts or Shakespeare do so for these reasons, but also because they enjoy showing off their erudite learning. Some of them, like Whiteley, struggle to distinguish between events they have *read* about from events they have *experienced* (she borrows ideas from a dozen teenage romance novels)—the "plagiarism" is innocent and inadvertent, though it may not seem that way to an outside reader.

One of the college courses I teach is an advanced course on writing research papers. When my AS students are given the task of gathering research from a variety of sources and then integrating that research into one cohesive essay, they often struggle with the process of synthesis. I see the same qualities in my students' work that I see in the literary works of the authors in this study: messiness; a "scrapbook" cut-and-paste quality to the manuscript; a tendency to quote or refer to other texts excessively; a naïve attitude toward plagiarism. Once again, outside help is very useful. Coaching and peer tutoring help immensely.

The writing process for people on the spectrum can sometimes be driven by obsession. Every writer in this study was highly focused on writing and dedicated a large percentage of his or her life to the enterprise. Their autism enabled them to "block out" the world at large and to focus exclusively on their writing (such as young Yeats's ability to write poems in a room crowded with his noisy family, not even hearing his name when they called to him). Such perseverance—and dedication—contributes to their ability to write well.

2. The Problem of Audience

While writing a novel or story or poem, the author with autism is less likely to be thinking about the reader's needs than a neurotypical writer would. This is a direct result of the way autism affects an individual's social sense: "Some researchers consider that the primary roots of autism lie in absence or impairment of built-in social instinct, present from birth" (Wing 65). Because some people with autism struggle with "theory of mind," or the ability to imagine what another person might be thinking, the problem of audience affects their writing in several ways.

For one thing, since the author lacks an understanding of how the reader will be thinking about the text, he or she cannot always provide a written work that provides accessible meaning. Communication fails. When examining Temple Grandin's writing, Oliver Sacks found "peculiar narrational gaps and discontinuities, sudden, perplexing changes of topic, brought about...by Temple's failure 'to appreciate that her reader does not share the important background information that she possesses'" (253). Thus the author with autism often creates a text that is hermetically sealed—it makes sense to him or her, but not to the reader. Some of Emily Dickinson's poems are indecipherable. Long stretches of *Moby Dick* do not seem to be designed with the reader in mind.

The confusion might also be deliberately introduced: Joyce's prose was at times so obfuscated—such as the prose in *Finnegans Wake*—that as he was writing he actually laughed out loud, imagining how stumped his readers would be when they read his novel. I recently read a story by a young woman with Asperger's Syndrome—it was a mish-mash of Japanese characters, domestic imagery, and French vocabulary that utterly defied interpretation, and yet she was confident in her writing and she was fond of her story because she knew exactly what the words meant *to her*—she didn't care what anyone else thought.

Another way that the writer with Asperger's Syndrome dismisses the audience is to produce a text that is not only by the author and for the author but also *about* the author. All of the authors in this study were heavily fixated on life-writing: autobiography, diary, or letter. Hans Christian Andersen wrote a new autobiography every ten years. Lewis Carroll kept fanatical lists about who came to dinner, who sat where, who ate what, and so on. Andersen, Thoreau, Carroll, Yeats, Whiteley, and others fastidiously wrote in a journal every day of their lives. Even their literary works are self-referential:

their poetry, non-fiction, and fiction writing all carry numerous and frequent references to the self. Without biographical research, the reader may not have the proper context for understanding the work and is thus excluded.

Writers on the spectrum often fit the stereotype of the author as a lonely, withdrawn, solitary artist. Because they struggle to understand social conventions and behaviors, they often find it stressful to be in the company of others, preferring to live and work alone. One thinks of Thoreau, a solitary figure in his rustic cabin in the woods; or Emily Dickinson, hiding from the world in her parents' house in Amherst. One thinks of Sherwood Anderson's desperate struggle to fit in with society; Joyce's self-imposed exile from Ireland. Bearing this in mind, the act of writing becomes a lifeline that seeks to connect the author to the outside world. "This is my letter to the world," Dickinson writes in a poem, "that never wrote to me." Asserting a sense of self in a literary text and sending that text out to be read by others is akin to tossing a note-filled bottle out to sea, hoping that someone will find it and read it. Emily Dickinson kept her poems hidden away in a trunk, and left instructions for the trunk's contents to be burned after her death. But since she did not destroy them herself, we can't help but wonder whether she was secretly hoping the poems would be read by somebody after she was safely out of the way.

3. Genre: Breaking the Rules

Psychologists have observed that people with Asperger's Syndrome are often "rule followers." Because life itself is often so chaotic and unpredictable, these individuals find comfort in schedules, routines, and rules that bring consistency and structure. Yet some AS people display a trait that is seemingly the opposite: they exhibit behavior that is defiant, oppositional, or non-conformist: they are "rule breakers," in a sense. Both kinds of attributes can be found in literature by writers on the spectrum. This paradox is expressed through the ways an author both uses *and* defies literary genres.

Many of the writers with autism that I have worked with or studied are drawn to writing in established genres that have pre-established conventions. The AS mind is said to think rigidly and "without imagination," thus finding comfort in beginning a writing project with some kind of template or form as a guide. Hans Christian Andersen wrote down many fairy tales that had been orally passed down for years and were already commonly known. Arthur Conan Doyle followed all of the conventions that Poe had established for detective fiction. Emily Dickinson used the American hymn as a form to guide her poems—her four-line stanzas often favored a 4-3-4-3 rhythm pattern and an ABAB rhyming scheme. James Joyce's *Ulysses* was written within the template of Homer's *Odyssey*—his character Leopold Bloom makes the same journey as the famous Greek traveler Odysseus.

But the writings, while based on forms, are anything but derivative. Far from it. The AS tendency toward defiance or non-conformist thinking comes into play here, causing the author to break genre conventions and bend the rules of a given form. Thus, Hans Christian Andersen did write his own, original fairy tales, and his own stories are strangely different from the ones that were passed down to him from folk culture. Andersen's little match girl is not saved by a fairy godmother in the end of his story—she freezes to death, all alone in a back alley. Emily Dickinson often "changes up" the traditional hymn rhythm by adding or subtracting syllables, and she defies the traditional rhyme scheme by using near rhyme, sight rhyme, or no rhyme at all. Joyce's story of an epic journey is set in downtown Dublin, not in a ship at sea.

The AS writer's stubborn resistance to using traditional forms in the expected way can lead to brilliant, highly original texts. Sherwood Anderson's *Winesburg, Ohio*, for example, was one of the very first books to present a novel-like plot in linked short stories. His innovation opened the door for more experimentation in the short story genre. Joyce's *Ulysses* crams every literary genre ever conceived of into one single novel—his innovative creativity placed him at the center of the *avant-garde*, modernist art movement.

Emily Dickinson's unconventional poems were too advanced for her generation (an editor told her to fix her "mistakes"), but opened the door for other modernist poets to follow her.

When Hans Asperger first started to observe ASD children, he observed that "unlike other children who struggled to progress from mechanical learning to original thought, the children he was describing were capable only of forming their own strategies. They could not, or did not, follow those used by their teachers" (Fitzgerald *Genesis* 28). Fitzgerald believes this creative stubbornness carries on into adulthood, and that this enhances innovation: "Persons with Asperger's syndrome generally have immature personalities and retain a child-like capacity. The retention of this child-like view helps their artistic work. They are also non-conformist, which creates novelty and interest" (*Genesis* 240). Literary history would be vastly different without these AS innovators.

4. *Autistic Narrative Strategies*

Professor Matthew K Belmonte's research explores how the autistic mind's lack of central coherence or executive function can impair the individual's ability to build a story or create a structured narrative. He argues that the cognitive factors that enable us to tell a story—how we integrate our observations, how we organize our thoughts, and how we process context—are all factors that autistic minds struggle with (3). Bernard Rimland agrees: "autistic persons experience life as an incoherent series of unconnected events" (xi). The details are there, but the story isn't. It's as though the autistic individual is looking through a shoe box filled with random handfuls of pictures and cannot organize them into a photograph album that tells a story.

As a result, writers on the spectrum often struggle with plot. Novelists are surely affected by this difficulty with narrative construction more than any other creative artists. The AS writers in this study show a marked resistance against the writing of novels, since novels typically require a sustained, organically whole fictional narrative. Sherwood Anderson wrote several unsuccessful novels before turning to short stories. Many of Melville's novels were not of good quality, and he found short fiction to be "more manageable" (Robertson-Lorant 329).

Consider *Alice in Wonderland*, for example. The events in this story are not organized according to the strategies that we would find in a typical novel. They do not follow from A to B to C in a logical fashion. There is no guiding "cause and effect" at work. The protagonist herself does not drive the events forward. Rather, the events of *Alice in Wonderland* appear in a random, haphazard order. The reader could shuffle all of the chapters like a deck of cards and the book would not be altered much. We follow Alice from random event to random event and enjoy the bumpy ride with the delight of children at an amusement park. A quality of randomness can be seen in other texts by authors with autism as well.

Michael Blastland argues that the profoundly autistic mind (as opposed to the mind with Asperger's Syndrome) does not possess any sense of narrative at all. For severely autistic people, he asserts, life is a series of "car crashes," random events that seemingly come from nowhere and cannot be predicted or understood: "They just don't see the psychological stitching between events that we see; and how do you create a narrative when there is only this succession of...car crashes?" (2). Is this lack of "back story" a bad thing? Not necessarily. Blastland considers the possibility that the life devoid of narrative is actually more realistic and authentic than the one with an artificial story fitted over it: "From one perspective, people with autism may understand life better than those of us who seek to impose narratives on its rather random events, because they have a better sense of how random things can be" (2). This would seem to suggest that an autistic person's writing, one that lacks a superimposed master narrative, is actually more realistic. Their stories are more realistic *because* they are more random.

Perhaps because sustained narratives are so hard to write, authors on the spectrum often turn to genres such as poetry, essays, or short stories, which, being shorter and more flexible forms of writing, seem better suited to the talents and cognitive abilities of an author with autism. In Sherwood Anderson's *Winesburg, Ohio*, short stories function as small vignettes of life in a Midwestern town. Emily Dickinson manages to pack a lot of imagery and meaning into each of her tiny poems. Thoreau's *Walden* works as a series of short essays, each self-contained. The desire to tell a story is there, but it has to be told in a different way. Critic Stuart Murray suggests that the neurotypical notion of narrative may itself be challenged as we become more sensitive to the way people with autism express their world view through language: "autism may in some way supply narratives of its own, stories and versions of life and its events that differ from those produced within majority culture" (5).

One substitute for the traditional plot that can be found in works by writers with autism is repetition. Repetition, like routine, is a tool that individuals with autism can use for coping with the uncertainty of life. Many of the AS individuals I know, including my son and my students, have certain words, phrases, or stories that they enjoy repeating over and over, despite the fact that the listener may not be very engaged in the repeated tellings. Valerie Paradiž has pointed out that Asperger's Syndrome might be the explanation behind Andy Warhol's repetitious portraits of Jackie, Chairman Mao, and Campbell soup cans (he also ate Campbell's soup for lunch every day). One of the most interesting examples of this verbal repetition must surely be Melville's short story "Bartleby," in which the main character repeats the expression "I would prefer not to" more than a dozen times.

Some writers with autism who want their voices to be heard by a wider audience have found it useful to engage an editor to help them organize their writing into a conventional narrative structure that will work for a neurotypical reader. Temple Grandin's book *Emergence* was written with the editing assistance of Margaret Scariano, who helped Temple pull her memories together into a cohesive narrative. Opal's childhood diary was pieced together and smoothed out with the help of editor Ellery Sedgwick. Emily Dickinson's poems found their way into print only after friends and family volunteered to edit and organize her work posthumously (sadly, her work lost some of its vitality in the process).

Even though many authors on the spectrum may find it challenging to shape a story into a narrative structure, the impulse to tell a story remains strong. In the case of Donna Williams, "By putting her chaotic life experiences on paper, in chronological order, Donna hoped to construct a coherent picture in her own mind of who she was" (Rimland xi). There is still the need to express the self. There is still the need to communicate with others. There is still the desire to create a beautiful work of art that will contribute to the accomplishments of humanity and will also outlive the self. Storytelling is a way to make sense out of our own lives, as Roger Schank observes: "Narrative is one of the most important ways in which we make sense of the world. It allows us to structure and remember events, structure time, and fit new events into a pattern" (Davis, et al 1). Or, as Yeats said, "A work of art is the social act of a solitary man" (Ellman 17).

5. Character Development

It seems reasonable to assume that in order for an author to create compelling, complex, realistic characters, he or she must have some understanding of human nature. Yet human nature is the one area of knowledge that individuals with AS struggle with the most. Psychologist Uta Frith observes: "Asperger syndrome individuals... do not seem to possess the knack of entering and maintaining intimate two-way personal relationships" (Sacks 275). Knowledge of what makes other people "tick and tock" is not instinctive to many people on the spectrum. They do not know how to read body language or facial expressions. They cannot fathom other people's motives or reasons for acting as they do. Social codes and group dynamics remain mysterious. Other people's humor is lost upon them. Sometimes a person with AS wants to make friends but doesn't know how.

A lack of knowledge of human nature makes creating characters problematic. AS writers use several strategies to get around this. One approach is to avoid creating fictional characters altogether. The author may use himself as a character, but otherwise writes about either abstract concepts or the non-human physical world. Thoreau focuses on philosophical issues and natural history rather than other people; the only person he really writes about is himself, the one person he feels he does understand: "I should not talk so much about myself if there were anybody else whom I knew as well," he explains. Emily Dickinson's poems are occasionally about people but are more often about objects such as flowers, birds, the ocean, trains, boats, the sun, and so on. Whiteley's childhood diary only makes observations about herself or animals; it says very little about her mother or sister.

Another approach to the problem of characterization is to present characters who lack depth or development but have an interesting surface that is flashy, glitzy, and glamorous. Many of the characters created by AS authors are superficial. Think of the fantasy characters found in Andersen's fairy tales: a mermaid, a princess, an emperor. Think of Yeats's reliance on folk heroes such as Cuchulain or Emer, or his fascination with fairies. Think of Carroll's Humpty Dumpty or Cheshire Cat. It seems to be true that simple but flashy characters appeal to readers with AS as well: leagues of young AS men would rather read *Lord of the Rings*, *Dungeons and Dragons* narratives, science fiction, or Japanese comic books than realistic novels featuring characters with complex emotional and social development.

One other strategy that writers on the spectrum use is to create characters who mirror themselves, characters who display traits of autism or Asperger's Syndrome. Herman Melville created an AS character named Bartleby who doesn't socialize with his office mates and doesn't appear to have a friend in the world. Bartleby's fate is a sad one—he dies alone and friendless in prison—suggesting that perhaps Melville was not satisfied with his own place in the world. Autistic characters created by autistic authors are extremely valuable indicators of what it's like to have this neurological difference. Their importance to both autistic and neurotypical audiences cannot be over-rated. My AS son may not have realized that Lewis Carroll was on the spectrum, but he did know that he loved *Alice in Wonderland* and that it was more important to him than any other book. From a very young age he would explain to me that he thought the book was written by "a smart person." Something about the book just resonated for him.

6. Setting: Creating the World through Detail

Three characteristics of Asperger's Syndrome nurture an author's tendency to sculpt a setting through multitudes of detail: acute sensory perception, exceptional memory, and perseveration on a special interest. Although some individuals with AS are plagued with serious vision problems, others do have the gift of phenomenal sight. Thoreau's friends marveled at his ability to spot small artifacts such as Indian arrow heads that nobody else could see. Opal Whiteley was also blessed with above-average visual perception and could see individual leaves on trees, caterpillars, and water droplets from far away. AS people can also have intense hearing abilities. Thunder troubled both Dickinson and Sherwood Anderson to the point of having to cover their ears when it was stormy. Dickinson was particularly sensitive to music. So was Hans Christian Andersen. A BBC radio announcer once commented that Yeats had the most acute hearing he'd ever encountered. Joyce had poor vision but exceptional hearing and an intense interest in music: his prose was aurally evocative.

Not only are some writers on the spectrum acutely aware of the kaleidoscope of sensory detail that surrounds them, but they also have a great capacity for remembering what they have seen and heard. Eidetic or "photographic" memory can give these individuals an endless supply of pigments with which to paint their canvas. Fitzgerald points out that although people with Asperger's Syndrome can have a weaker capacity for remembering experiences and events, they usually have an excellent memory for facts (*Autism*

47). Strong perception coupled with exceptional memory allows the writers mentioned above, and others, to faithfully re-create on the page what they have experienced in life. AS writers tend to develop setting through the accumulation of detail upon detail upon detail. Fitzgerald observed an "Asperger type of approach—the artist builds up his drawings or sculpture out of separate parts, as one would build [with] bricks" (*Genesis* 204).

Sometimes the number of details in a paragraph can overwhelm the reader. The authors become infatuated with recording the details of their story, and they lose track of the story itself because of the neurological compulsion to "focus on detail with massive curiosity and total immersion" (*Genesis* 239). Description becomes more important than narrative, dialogue, or exposition. Plot and character fade to the background. Setting is privileged over all else.

An unusual focus on details could also be triggered by an autistic person's tendency to focus and perseverate on objects of special interest. Thoreau's love for Walden Pond inspired him to record every kind of detail imaginable from water color to water temperature to water depth for many months. *Moby Dick* is filled with unusual details that Melville remembered from his years at sea. Opal Whiteley was fixated on French royal families and she includes many references to them in her childhood diary, even though she grew up in the woods of Oregon country.

Author Daniel Tammet, who has Asperger's Syndrome, explained that his fascination with descriptive writing began at a young age: "around the age of eight I wrote compulsively across long reams of computer paper, often writing for hours at a time, covering sheet after sheet of paper with tightly knit words" (44). As an adult looking back, he recognized that his style of writing was somewhat unusual in that it did not contain characters or plot:

> The stories I wrote, from what I can remember of them, were descriptively dense—a whole page might be taken up in describing the various details of a single place or location,

> its colors, shapes, and textures. There was no dialogue, no emotions. Instead I wrote of long, weaving tunnels far underneath vast, shimmering oceans, of cragged rock caves and towers climbing high into the sky. (44)

When he writes his autobiography as an adult, years later, he is still interested in giving the reader very precise, specific descriptions of the objects he encounters. This appears to be a common tendency among writers on the spectrum.

7. Rich Use of Symbolism

Many writers who have autism rely on symbolism to infuse their work with rich significance and beauty. The symbols are used to convey meaning in an indirect way that is more subtle than direct exposition and seems to be a good fit for people who struggle with language and communication. Several researchers (including Kristina Chew) have recently observed that autistic thinking tends to be "associational" thinking—that is, one mental image leads to another that leads to another. This might be why symbolic expression comes naturally to so many of them.

Many autobiographies written by people diagnosed with AS present symbols that specifically refer to autism. Temple Grandin wrote about the glass door that separated her from other people and from the rest of the outside world. Donna Williams wrote about the mirror that showed her another version of the world, including another version of herself. Liane Holliday Willey wrote about the walls, paths, and bridges that either blocked her access to other people or allowed her to make a connection with them. Dawn Prince-Hughes wrote about the cage of her autism that kept her separated from society, but she also explained that later on this cage became her refuge as she learned to enjoy and celebrate her own unique identity. Prime numbers were important to Daniel Tammet, who appreciated their rare, distinctive beauty.

Author Valerie Paradiž, who first wrote about her autistic son Elijah (in *Elijah's Cup*) before realizing that she too was on the autism spectrum, described Elijah's early, mysterious seizures with poetic language that rings with haunting symbolic beauty:

> Is a seizure a flower? Is it a thorn sticking in the mind? Does it hurt? Is it a color? Is it a long journey? Is it the deepest of isolations, like a solitary poppy, emerging, orange and paper thin, in the quiet garden? (17)

Her son's epileptic seizures are repeatedly represented by the image of a blooming flower, a surprising image for such a frightening and dangerous occurrence. In describing her own personal feelings of sorrow and hopelessness, she uses a different kind of metaphor:

> Auditory anchor, auditory anchor, falling down to the bottom of the sea. We are sinking, sinking softly. How far does a voice travel when it's under water? How far can it recede from the surface events? Where in these depths is the telling juncture, the juncture of identity? Is it between the silence and the song? Between Elijah and me? We have gone all the way to the bottom. The anchor has landed, and in between the silence and the song, my son is asking me to become a different woman. (22)

The sadness she feels while watching her son suffer, combined with the frustration and depression she feels about her new role as the mother of a child with autism, finds expression in a watery landscape that pulls her to a watery death. The anchor is a metaphor for despair. As she sinks deeper and deeper, she loses the voice that she had previously used for singing Elijah to sleep. In the process of becoming an anchor for Elijah, she drowns and loses herself.

Writers who were working before AS was recognized as a specific neurological condition also wrote about their differences through the vehicle of symbol. Hans Christian Andersen's fairy tales were rich with fanciful characters who symbolized his feelings of alienation and separateness from other people, including the lonely ugly duckling, the lovelorn little mermaid, and the neglected little match girl.

Herman Melville, who displayed many traits of Asperger's Syndrome, created Bartleby, an AS character who was isolated from all other people. In the story, Bartleby's autism was symbolically depicted through the setting—his office was on "Wall" Street, a wall separated him from his fellow employees, his desk faced a wall, and the only window in his office faced another brick wall outside. Bartleby never seems to go anywhere. He never leaves his office. This must be the most depressing symbolic interior landscape ever developed in a literary text.

Houses and buildings are described by Sherwood Anderson with language that suggests an autistic architecture in *Winesburg, Ohio.* There is Wing Biddlebaum's decayed, broken down house on the edge of town, surrounded by weeds. Enoch Robinson lives alone in a one-room, oddly shaped apartment in the middle of metropolitan New York. A cramped apartment above a store that is filled with useless, unwanted junk is the home of Elmer Cowley. Anderson's misfit characters live in structures that emphasize their difference, their isolation, their alienation, and their despair.

Nature, too, provides a landscape that is symbolic of the autistic person's separation from the neurotypical mainstream culture. Emily Dickinson's repeated trope of a little boat ("my bark went down at sea") lost in a vast, vast ocean suggests her feelings of isolation. Yeats's recurring image of a lake island (land surrounded by water surrounded by land surrounded by water), such as the Lake Isle of Innisfree, also portrays a feeling of apartness. Andersen's characters are often surrounded by frigid water, snow, or ice. They sometimes die from cold.

Communicating ideas and feelings through rich symbolism is a special gift for writers with Asperger's Syndrome. It may be that this kind of indirect presentation of the self is easier to manage  than blatantly revealing oneself through direct language. It may be easier to describe a bizarre apartment for a fictional character than to say "I don't fit in." In *Nobody Nowhere*, Donna Williams provides an interesting and useful analysis of her own method for communicating her emotions, which involves using symbolic gesture rather than words. For her, gestures such as two fingers held together, or toes scrunched up, carry meaning and are an "effort to communicate." She explains that gestures like this are the best way for her to explain what is going on in "her world." She knows that all people have feelings, including those on the spectrum, despite the popular notion that they do not. Children with autism "have feeling, but it has developed in isolation and can't be verbalized in the usual way, and most people cannot hear with anything other than their ears" (210). Symbolism, the oldest form of human communication, serves autistic writers—and readers—very well.

8. Theme

When an author with autism writes about his or her place among others in society, a theme of alienation prevails in these stories. This theme is strongest among the authors who were never diagnosed with ASD. They know that something about them is different. They feel that there is something wrong with them. They may or may not try to fit in, but if they do try to make a friend, they find that it isn't easy. There's no ignoring the messages of loneliness, sadness, or despair that permeate much of the literature. One thinks of Hans Christian Andersen's cold, wet, frozen characters struggling against the elements with no one to help them. One thinks of Bartleby, dying of a broken heart, all alone, in prison. Or Alice, swimming in a lake of her own tears. One thinks of Sherwood Anderson's sad, oddball characters sitting by themselves in dilapidated shacks and upstairs apartments. The underlying message, again and again, is this: I am different and the world has rejected me.

In more recent times, when an autistic writer is diagnosed and learns about what it means to be on the spectrum, he or she starts to feel better about who he is. The anguish, then, is tempered with an expression of self-acceptance and even pride. The five autobiographies included in the final chapter of this study reveal the same pattern every time. Diagnosis leads to self-understanding, which can eventually lead to acceptance. Temple Grandin writes about the joy she has found in working with animals. Dawn Prince-Hughes celebrates her success with domestic partnership and motherhood. Donna Williams describes leaving behind her life as a homeless person to become a proud home owner. Themes of triumph over adversity can be found in works by authors who have autism: I may be different, but I can focus on my strengths and learn to accept myself.

9. Rich Language

Mathematicians love numbers; painters love color; writers love words—writers with AS really *really* love words. Language is their obsession, their passion, and their joy. Even as children, the AS authors in this study were enamored with the word, whether written or spoken. As a little girl in grade school, Opal Whiteley recorded being mesmerized by the "spell of the words" as she used crayons to record her thoughts on pieces of recycled butcher paper and old envelopes. Poly-syllabic words such as "screw-tin-eyes" or "at-ten-chuns" especially caught her interest. Yeats's father observed that when Willie discovered a word he liked, he would walk in circles around the house repeating the word over and over, eyes closed, flapping his arms. Dawn Prince-Hughes thought words like "sssssilver dollllar" had a magical quality when she repeatedly wrapped her mouth around them.

Most of these writers were hyper-lexic, reading far more books than the people around them, even as children. As a girl, Whiteley checked out hundreds of books from the Oregon State Library in Salem, angering the librarian by keeping most of them indefinitely. As a young woman at the University of Oregon, she checked out more library books than any other student. When Whiteley was an elderly woman put into a mental asylum in England, her tiny

London apartment was so crowded with tall stacks of books that nobody could get through the rooms. As a boy, Lewis Carroll loved reading about religion, English literature, and mathematics. Hans Christian Andersen spent so much time reading he often forgot to eat—as a child he memorized entire acts of Shakespeare, reciting them as he walked down the streets of Odense. Thoreau begged Harvard to stretch the limit of library books one could check out so he could indulge his appetite for reading. All of this reading no doubt contributed to the authors' rich use of language.

Many people with AS have a facility for learning languages, and several of these authors were poly-lingual. James Joyce could speak a dozen foreign languages, and could learn a new one after a very short exposure to it. Thoreau quickly picked up French, Spanish, German, Italian, Greek, Latin, and bits of Sanskrit and Native American languages. Autobiographer Daniel Tammet could speak many languages including English, Lithuanian, Romanian, Welsh, Esperanto, Spanish, French, and German, and was able to teach himself Icelandic—on a dare—in seven days. Dawn Prince-Hughes understood the communication patterns of gorillas. Whiteley enjoyed zigzagging between English and French, between high diction and childish prattle, between Catholic ritual and a conversation with a pig.

Daniel Tammet also created a brand new language from scratch—it gave him great pleasure to speak and write in a language, "Mänti," that existed only for him. Donna Williams recalled that as a child "I developed a language of my own" (29). Joyce loved to make up new words. Jonathan Swift gave us the words "Yahoo" and "Lilliputian." If writers on the spectrum can't find the word they need, these wordsmiths often make it up. Researcher Tony Attwood noted that:

> Some individuals with Asperger's have the ability to create their own form of language (known as neologisms). He gives as examples a girl's description of the ankle as the "wrist of my foot" and ice cubes as "water bones." Dr. Attwood describes

> this ability as "one of the endearing and genuinely creative aspects of Asperger's Syndrome." (as quoted by Tammet 169)

In this sense, the AS person is the supreme inventor of idiom. Rather than dismissing their made up phrases as gibberish, we would be rewarded for making the effort to de-code them, just as we would be willing to do with difficult poetry:

> The word "idiom" is from the classical Greek *idiotes*, "private citizen"; a cognate word, "idiolect," refers to a private language. Due to the unusual use of words and syntax, the language of an autistic person can be classified as a language for a community of one, as a private language. Rather than seeing this language as "incomprehensible," we can interpret it by trying to understand the "system" the user has created, just as, to read a poem, we need to decode the poet's use of tropes, of metaphor, tone, meter. (Chew 4)

The Lewis Carroll poem "Jabberwocky" is just one delightful example of an idiolect—children everywhere (and adults) enjoy playing around with these syllables.

The AS writers studied here were willing to break the boundaries of convention. They followed the rules of grammar when they wanted to, but didn't hesitate to use fragments or run on sentences if they felt like it. Emily Dickinson used more dashes than any poet before or after her. She didn't care if her poetry followed a conventional rhyme or rhythm pattern—even though ignoring these conventions made it impossible for her to publish much during her lifetime. Joyce refused to use quotation marks for dialogue because he didn't like the way they looked. He also insisted on describing normal human body functions in his writing, even though the government labeled his writing obscene. If Sherwood Anderson couldn't describe a person, the narrator would just admit it to the reader. Fitzgerald agrees that AS writers have a flair for doing something different: "There is no doubt that in a literary sense there is something distinctive and unusual in their literary works" (*Genesis* 28). The Aspergen willingness to depart from the normal, to ignore academic conventions of writing, served these writers well as they blazed new trails in literature. These writers were all in love with language, and this passion led to a richness of musical description and exposition that makes the reader's heart sing along.

This book is dedicated to the exploration of autistic writing. Each chapter focuses on one specific author and, after a brief look at the author's life story and AS traits, takes a closer look at the poems, stories, novels, and essays in order to determine how autism shaped them. People who are interested in literature will find here a new approach to understanding how an author's mindset can influence his or her writing. While psychoanalytical criticism can offer some interesting insights into literature, sometimes it just doesn't offer an accurate or helpful explanation. I do not believe the explanation that Carroll was writing about his fear of sexuality or that Sherwood Anderson was working through his oedipal complex in his writing or that Hans Christian Andersen's fairy tales reflect "castration anxiety." I believe that these writers wrote what they wrote (and wrote *how* they wrote) because of their place on the autism spectrum. People who are interested in autism will find here an introduction to articulate and creative voices that have much to teach us about their world if only we will listen. This book will give you a new way to read books you are already familiar with—or else will introduce you to writers you will surely want to read.

Works Cited

Belmonte, Matthew K. "Human, but More So: What the Autistic Brain Tells Us about the Process of Narrative." Autism and Representation Conference Proceedings. Case Western Reserve University, Cleveland Ohio. October 28-30, 2005. http://cwru.edu/affil/sce/Texts_2005/Autism%20and%20Representation%20 Belmonte.htm. Used by permission.

Blastland, Michael. "In Sickness and in Hope: A Conversation with Neil Vickers and Francesca Happé." *Prospect* Sept. 2007: 1-3. http://www.prospectmagazine.co.uk/2007/oq/insicknessandinhope.

Chew, Kristina. "Fractioned Idiom: Poetry and the Language of Autism." Autism and Representation Conference Proceedings. Case Western Reserve University, Cleveland, Ohio. October 28-30, 2005. http://cwru.edu/affil/sce/Texts_2005/Autism%20and%20Representation%20Chew.htm. Used by permission.

Davis, Megan, et al. *Towards an Interactive System Facilitating Therapeutic Narrative Elicitation in Autism.* University of Hertfordshire. http://homepages.feis.herts.ac.uk.

Ellman, Richard. *Yeats: The Man and the Masks.* NY: Norton, 1978.

Fitzgerald, Michael. *Autism and Creativity: Is There a Link Between Autism in Men and Exceptional Ability?* NY: Taylor and Francis, 2004.

---. *The Genesis of Artistic Creativity: Asperger's Syndrome and the Arts.* London: Jessica Kingsley Publishers, 2005.

Jackson, Luke. *Freaks, Geeks, and Asperger's Syndrome.* London: Jessica Kingsley Publishers, 2002.

Murray, Stuart. *Representing Autism: Culture, Narrative, Fascination.* Liverpool: Liverpool University Press, 2008.

Paradiž, Valerie. *Elijah's Cup.* New York: The Free Press, 2002.

Rimland, Bernard. Introduction to Donna Williams's *Nobody Nowhere.* NY: Avon, 1992.

Robertson-Lorant, Laurie. *Melville.* NY: Clarkson Potter Publishers, 1996.

Sacks, Oliver. *An Anthropologist on Mars: Seven Paradoxical Tales.* New York: Vintage Books, 1995.

Tammet, Daniel. *Born on a Blue Day: A Memoir.* NY: Simon and Schuster, 2006.

Williams, Donna. *Nobody Nowhere.* NY: Avon, 1992.

Wing, Lorna. *The Autistic Spectrum: A Parents' Guide to Understanding and Helping Your Child.* Berkeley, CA: Ulysses Press, 2001.

CHAPTER TWO

Hans Christian Andersen

Hans Christian Andersen and Asperger's Syndrome

Danish author Hans Christian Andersen (1805–1875) is best known for his well-loved fairy tales, including "The Ugly Duckling," "The Little Mermaid," and "The Emperor's New Clothes." The story of his own life, in fact, reads something like a fairy tale. He was born to a poor couple who lived in a small cottage in the slums of Odense. His father was a shoemaker, a dreamy intelligent man who loved to read and loved to tell stories to his son. His mother, who had been a beggar as a child, was a washerwoman who kept house and took care of Hans Christian. She was illiterate and very superstitious.

Andersen's family situation was unorthodox. His grandmother sometimes worked as a prostitute and sometimes worked in the lunatic asylum. She had three illegitimate children by three different men. His grandfather was insane. Andersen had an older half sister, Karen Marie, who was illegitimate. When Andersen was a boy, his father joined Napoleon's army and went off to fight—after he came back, he became sick and died. After his father died, the family was so poor that young Andersen sometimes had to beg for money for food. His mother turned to alcoholism and eventually died of tuberculosis.

Andersen left home at the age of 14 to try to make a living in the big city of Copenhagen. His dream was to work as a dancer, singer, or actor, and he was certainly bold enough to believe he could do it even if he did lack talent. Wealthy citizens of Copenhagen felt sorry for the homely and awkward teenager, and they set up a fellowship to support him while he finished his schooling. He had many odd behaviors, all due to his Asperger's Syndrome (AS). He would walk through the streets with a clumsy gait and his eyes closed, or else would recite Shakespeare as he walked (his eidetic memory allowed him to memorize entire plays). He brazenly presented himself to leaders in the town and asked them to find him a job as a professional actor or dancer. He would lecture people on odd topics, such as the time he walked into the poor house and started telling the old women about body organs and their functions. His social skills were rough and very clumsy, but he was always sincere and somehow likeable.

Despite being dyslexic, he started to write creatively while in school. He tried out several genres, including poetry, fiction, and drama. As an adult, he kept a journal every day and was a manic letter writer. He also wrote a new autobiography every few years. He struggled excessively with the process of writing his life history and as a result each autobiography is different, as though he could not find a version of his life that made sense to him.

Once he turned his pen to fairy tales, his talent blossomed and he gained world-wide recognition. His fame granted him entrance to homes of the aristocracy and even royalty. He went on reading tours around Europe and was highly esteemed by children and adults alike. The ending of his life story puts one in mind of his most famous fairy tale: the ugly duckling had turned into a swan. To this day he remains one of the world's most beloved authors.

Although Andersen was born years before the word "autism" was used, it is clear that Andersen had Asperger's Syndrome. According to the research of Michael Fitzgerald, Andersen displayed so many symptoms of AS that it is "very likely" he was impacted by it. Fitzgerald identifies the following characteristics of AS, all of which describe Andersen: social impairments, narrow interests, repetitive routines, speech and language peculiarities, and non-verbal communication problems (*Autism* 28). But Andersen also had the beneficial AS traits of hyperlexia, ability to focus, persistence, and high intelligence. The combination of all of these qualities influenced his writing considerably. An examination of his fairy tales reveals a direct correlation between his place on the spectrum and the writing of his stories.

An Autistic Writing Process

The writing process Andersen employed for writing his autobiographies was very frustrating for him. Rough drafts reveal paragraphs and pages written, scribbled out, re-written, and scribbled out again. At one point he even tried pasting up a collage of different bits—including paragraphs written by other people—and asked for editing assistance from a trusted friend. The act of writing his life story was very challenging for him and took its toll, causing him both psychological and physical stress:

> Let me tell you that it has not been an easy task to gather everything together in my mind, to compress it onto paper, and to do it in a single effort of writing it down. I am also certain that this work has affected my whole nervous system as much as the heat has. (Jens Andersen 336)

Some of the anxiety no doubt resulted from the agony he felt over deciding what to reveal and what to hide, what was memory and what was fantasy, what was memorable and what was trivial. The process of converting specific details and discreet facts into a smooth, coherent narrative was overwhelming. People with Asperger's Syndrome are often good at handling detail, but not so good at managing the "big picture." Acknowledging that the manuscript was something of a jumbled mess, he asked his lifelong friend Edvard Collin to edit the manuscript for him. In a sense, Andersen was also asking Edvard to edit his very identity: *Am I ok? Am I good enough? Do I please you?* In making a fairy tale out of his life, Andersen transformed himself from a man into a "main character" (Jens Andersen 333).

In contrast, once he began working in the fairy tale genre, the writing process became much smoother and his rough drafts reveal a smooth penmanship and a more confident author. Andersen began by borrowing familiar stories and writing them down in his own voice, as though he were telling the story to a child. Like several other writers on the spectrum (such as Yeats and Joyce), he seemed to work best when starting with familiar material, and then moving from that to unexplored territory. For ideas he turned to *The Arabian Nights*, European folk tales, Jonathan Swift, Cervantes, and other sources (*Stories*, various notes). As he gained confidence over his ability to write, he began to invent more original material. Some of his best works, including "The Ugly Duckling" and "The Little Mermaid," were drawn purely from his own experiences and imagination.

Andersen's Fairy Tales

Andersen did not meet with much critical success in writing poetry, plays, or novels. These genres were not a good fit for him—his writing was considered to be superficial, immature, and unoriginal. Critics faulted him for creating heroes who were obvious stand-ins for himself: young geniuses struggling for recognition but finding only rejection. When Andersen turned to writing fairy tales, however, these writing "faults," some of them stemming from his Asperger's Syndrome, became assets instead. In fairy tales, superficial character development is not a problem, as characters are known by size, occupation, or even birth order. Immature presentation is not a flaw, as fairy tales written for children have a special naïve charm to them. Drawing upon folk tales that are already familiar to the audience is not seen as derivative, but rather heightens the cultural resonance of a fairy tale. Andersen's tendency to feature himself in his writing also worked out very well in the stories that he crafted. Fairy tales turned out to be the ideal genre for a writer with Asperger's Syndrome, allowing Andersen to channel his own thinking pattern and writing style into a format that showcased his creative talent.

Fairy tales were enjoying a popular resurgence at the time that Andersen was writing. Other ethnographers (such as Jacob and Wilhelm Grimm, Joseph Jacobs, Jørgen Moe, and later on W. B. Yeats) were collecting the folk tales of their nations at about this time, but Andersen not only re-shaped the old stories he'd heard as a child, he also wrote new ones created from his own experiences and imagination. This leap into creating original tales was a catalyst for his genius: "Andersen was the first writer to treat this peasant form as a literary genre and to invent new tales which entered the collective unconsciousness with the same mythic power as the ancient, anonymous ones" (Wullschlager 2).

A close examination of Andersen's fairy tales reveals much about the way an autistic mind translates observation and imagination into language, and language into story. His place on the spectrum made the genre of fairy tales the perfect expression of his unique creative genius. His AS impacted his narrative structure, description, characterization, use of symbol, and also the way he portrayed his feelings about himself and his differences from other people.

Autism and Narrative Structure

1. Randomness

Individuals on the autistic spectrum can have a difficult time processing unexpected cause and effect relationships. Unanticipated change is a hard thing for them to manage. Psychologist Lorna Wing identifies an autistic individual's "inability to put together all kinds of information derived from past memories and present events, to make sense of experiences, to predict what is likely to happen in the future, and to make plans." She concludes that "people with autistic disorders...find it difficult to organize themselves in time and in space" (4). For a writer, such cognitive processing skills are necessary for fashioning a cohesive narrative or plot within a fictional story. A person who does not see an over-arcing narrative in the events of his life will either find it challenging to create one in his stories or else will find a different way of telling his story. Since an autistic person's perception of his experiences has a more "random" quality to it, his stories often do, too. Neurologist Oliver Sacks made a related observation about the writing style of author Temple Grandin: "There were strange discontinuities (people injected suddenly into the narrative without warning, for instance); casual reference to incidents of which the reader had no knowledge; and sudden, perplexing changes of topic" (14). He attributes this to Grandin's lack of "theory of mind." The same can be said of Andersen's writing.

Many of Andersen's tales, especially the lesser known ones, are based on plots governed by random chance rather than by cause and effect. In the story "The Sweethearts," for example, a series of external, arbitrary events dictates the terms of a romantic relationship. Andersen humorously features two toys—a spinning top and a ball—as the main characters in this goofy love affair. The top and the ball first meet when they are thrown together in a drawer, and the top immediately declares his undying love for the ball. When someone bounces the ball, she suddenly disappears and he is very sad without her. When someone spins the top, he falls out of a window. When they bump into each other five years later in a garbage heap outside, he snubs her because she has not weathered well. The top is found by a human and brought back into the house where he lives happily ever after—the ball remains sad and alone in the garbage heap outside. A twist of fate has separated them, and nothing they do can remedy this.

The events of this story, at least so far as the top can fathom them, are random events that he does not control or understand. In a more conventional story, the author would explain why the ball bounced away, and how her disappearance changed the top's life. We would learn why the top had to spin out of a window, and how it affected him. We would learn why he cannot stay true to her, and why he prefers to snub her in the end.

The top in this story resembles Andersen, who was often frustrated by love. At the time that he was writing this story, he was in love with a beautiful young lady named Riborg Voight, who did not love him in return. She was in love with someone else, the son of a pharmacist—but that didn't stop Andersen from trying to impress her. In the story, the top shows off for his girl by spinning around, faster and faster. Anyone who has worked with autistic children will recognize this "spinning" as a typical gesture of either stress or excitement:

> "Look at me!" he said to the Ball [while spinning madly]. "What do you say now? Don't you want to be sweethearts? We're made for each other. You jump and I dance. Nobody could be happier than the two of us." (*Stories* 153)

Unfortunately, the Ball "disappears," which only intensifies his fixation: "Just because he could not have her, he loved her even more; it seemed odd to him that she had gone and chosen someone else" (*Stories* 153). The top has been rejected, and isn't sure why. This happened to Andersen several times in his life, when he would develop an interest in a young lady (or man) who would not return the favor. He was always bewildered by rejection. Since he could not fathom other people's motives, their actions seemed arbitrary and mysterious to him. His characters, similarly, either act without any obvious motivation or else in response to random outside forces beyond their control.

2. Repetition/Ritual

Because reality seems so chaotic and unpredictable to people with AS, they are often reassured by repeating activities or behaviors that give pleasure or comfort (Wing 23). Individuals on the autism spectrum often turn to repetition or ritual because it allows them to predict what will happen next, and the familiarity created by repetition leads to feelings of security. Andersen's stories contain numerous examples of repetition. Instead of crafting a plot that crescendos unavoidably toward a climactic finish, Andersen often shapes his narratives with measures of repetition instead.

In "The Emperor's New Clothes," for example, the entire story is built upon the way various characters respond to the mysterious fabric, and with one exception every character responds to it in the same way. When the characters are shown the non-existent cloth and asked to comment on it, each one is unable to trust his own senses. They fear they will be ridiculed for failing to see what "everyone else" can see, so for protection they repeat what they have heard the swindlers say: the characters mimic phrases rather than responding in a spontaneous fashion. The old minister, when asked for an opinion, thinks to himself: "Could I possibly be stupid? I never thought so. No one must know. Am I incompetent?" (*Stories* 107). He responds by agreeing that the cloth is "quite charming." Just as the minister repeated what the swindlers said, the bureaucrat repeats what the minister said, and so on until the Emperor himself repeats the hollow words of praise. Andersen builds the story through the repetitiveness that individuals with AS are known to enjoy and prefer.

In "The Little Matchgirl" (1845), Andersen also explores the autistic love of repetition and ritual to build his story. The heroine is a lonely outsider who is not allowed to enter the houses of the neighborhood, but must wander from street to street selling matches. She can only solve her problems short term: by lighting a match, she can momentarily warm her fingers—and she can also "see" heartening visions as well. The lighting of the matches becomes a ritual that protects her from grim reality. She gains power each time she strikes one, and the repeated ritual creates visions with greater intensity and pleasure. *Wsssbhbt*, one match brings her warmth. *Wsssbhbt*, another match makes her warmer. *Wsssbhbt*, a third match sustains her warmth. The rhythm of the text is built around this repetitive action. These matches also allow her to see some amazing things: the things that other people have, that she will always lack: a warm home, a tasty dinner, a Christmas tree, and a grandmother who loves her. The matches serve as a talisman to ward away her bad fortune. As long as she can repeat the ritual, she can stay warm and content. But when the last match goes out, she freezes to death on a snowy night because the magic ritual has ended.

3. *Obsession with a Special Interest*

Hans Asperger identified the recurring trait of "intense circumscribed interest in particular subjects such as railway timetables" in the autistic individuals he studied (Wing xiii). AS individuals like Andersen are known to fixate on "special interests" that catch their fancy. Several of his fairy tales are structured around one character's intense desire to possess a certain object or perseverate on a single idea. The character moves toward the obsession like a steel penny toward a magnet and the story only ends after the character either possesses the object of desire or is "cured" of his or her unnaturally strong wish.

"The Nightingale" (1844) explores the Aspergen fixation with gadgets. An Emperor hears about a famous nightingale that lives somewhere in his kingdom, and desires to hear it. The bird sings and the Emperor shows his appreciation. But when someone gives the Emperor a *mechanical* nightingale made of jewel-encrusted gold that can sing as well as the real bird, the Emperor is bedazzled by it. In the classic pattern of a person with Asperger's Syndrome, the Emperor becomes mesmerized by this glittery gadget. He makes it sing 32 times, and doesn't grow tired of it. He perseverates on the bird to the exclusion of everything around him, including the authentic bird that really does care for him. This is similar to ASD boys whose lives are consumed by hand-held video games, to the point where they prefer spending hours alone, with their gadgets, to playing with other children. Eventually the mechanical bird breaks, the Emperor gets sick, and people start to wonder what happened to the real bird. The only thing that can save the Emperor in the end is the realization that the authentic song of a warm-blooded bird is better than the artificial bliss induced by a gadget. Fortunately, he figures this out. The autistic character is able to break off his fixation and move toward emotional complexity—only then can the story end.

We see the same pattern of obsession in "The Red Shoes." Karen is a poor little girl who is obsessed with owning a pair of red shoes. Once she finally possesses a fine pair of patent-leather red shoes, she can't stop admiring them and preening in them. Her fixation on the shoes distracts her from her proper duties, such as obeying her elders and praying in church, and in the end she is punished: the shoes take on a life of their own and they start to dance uncontrollably, dancing the poor girl all over town. Not until her feet are amputated and her heart undergoes a serious repentance does the story draw to its conclusion—she dies and is brought to heaven, away from the evil red shoes. The story swirls like a hurricane around the girl's obsession and then finally dies away. The shoes, like the mechanical nightingale, hold the story together more than any rising or falling action.

Description: Attention to Surfaces/The Superficial

It is well documented that individuals on the autistic spectrum pay close attention to surfaces and the external appearance of objects. Children with autism are especially fascinated by bright lights, sparkles, moving things, parts of things, objects with interesting textures, and objects that make noise. To a person on the autistic spectrum, the outward appearance of an object is often more important than the object's history, cultural value, or emotional significance. Given the choice between a shiny pop bottle that makes noise when you drop it on the floor or the gift of an heirloom teddy bear from loving grandparents, the child who has autism will more likely want the pop bottle.

This was true in Andersen's case. As a child he enjoyed performing puppet shows for his family, but was happiest when cutting and sorting bits of brightly colored shiny fabrics. He enjoyed quiet nights with his friends the Collin family, but was also bedazzled by invitations to "glitterati" events that put wealth, fame, and pedigree on display. People who knew him thought his fascination with the outward trappings of beauty and fame was a "sickly character flaw" (Jens Andersen 287), but I see it as a function of his autism. Understanding this aspect of Andersen's perceptual process—being drawn toward a flashy external appearance—helps to explain why he was less successful writing literary novels and more successful working in the folk tradition. His novels lacked emotional depth, subtlety, and sophistication, but these are not requirements for successful fairy tales. Fairy tales are all about surface and sparkle and shine.

The story "Thumbelisa," for example (more popularly called "Thumbelina" in the US), perfectly demonstrates the autistic writing trait of privileging surface appearances over substance. The main characters in the story are divided into two camps—the beautiful (Thumbelisa, the sparrow, the prince) and the ugly (the toad, the beetle, and the mole). As in all fairy tales, the characters' appearances are the only clues we have as to their inherent goodness or badness. Thumbelisa likes the "beautiful little bird" and the "beautiful" prince. Her own beauty is the measure of her worth throughout the story. She dislikes the "repulsive toad" and the "ugly mole" with his "dark house." Much of the language of the story is devoted to descriptions of surface details, including ribbons, clothing, furniture, blankets, dishes, flowers, leaves, and butterflies. Andersen does not provide information about Thumbelisa's relationship with her mother, her attitude toward herself, or the significance of anything in her life or anything else in the story, for that matter. He does not explore any character's emotional makeup or map any growth or progress. Thumbelisa doesn't change—she is the same character in the first paragraph as she is in the last. As long as everything has an interesting appearance, nothing else seems to matter. Andersen never peaks below the surface—and since this is a fairy tale, we know that we should not ask him to. When Andersen used this "superficial" writing style in his longer literary pieces, it wasn't a successful strategy—but his attention to external appearances works very well in fairy tales.

Andersen's Characterization

It is surely a common tendency for a literary writer to model one or more characters after himself or herself. When the author has a mental illness or a neurological impairment, a close examination of the author's "shadow self" character can be very revealing as to the nature of the human psyche. Andersen could not resist pouring himself into nearly everything he wrote, even the most fantastical fairy tale. Not surprisingly, nearly all of Andersen's main characters display one or more traits of Asperger's Syndrome. A close study of these characters reveals that he was acutely aware of his difference from other people—and that he had mixed feelings about this difference.

The Little Mermaid: An Alienated, Autistic Self

In many of his stories the female character is the one who is most like him in presenting autistic characteristics. In "The Little Mermaid" (1837), for example, a mermaid leaves home to explore the big wide world, just as Andersen left Odense for Copenhagen, and she discovers that she is very different from the others. "She was a strange child, quiet and thoughtful," just like young Andersen. She longed to visit the big city, and to see "the lights blink[ing] like hundreds of stars…the hustle and bustle of carriages and people" (*Stories* 80). She finds a group of small human children playing at the beach, and she wants to play with them, "but they were frightened and ran away," leaving her alone (*Stories* 83). After falling in love with a prince, she has to face the sad truth: she is an outsider. "The thing that's so wonderful in the sea, your fish tail, is considered hideous up on land" (*Stories* 91), she is told. Like the AS child on the playground, she wants to fit in and join the others, but finds it isn't easy. She is rejected merely for being herself.

In order for her to grow legs and thus be "normal," she makes a bargain with a sea-witch and purchases normality with her voice. The trade-off costs her dearly. Andersen also understood that he needed to adopt a certain persona in order to be accepted by others:

> Andersen...played to his audience, and was soon a local celebrity. It assured his rise up the social ladder, but it also marked the start of a process of psychological self damage, of living a life in which he always felt he had to act a part, until in the end he was no longer certain who he really was. (Wullschlager 28)

This echoes the way some individuals who have autism feel that they must sacrifice their natural selves in order to earn acceptance by neurotypical others. The mermaid's longing for legs may be the best way she can find for "passing" or "fitting in" with the crowd that she admires. It might be easy to criticize the compromise, but Donna Williams defends this familiar strategy of individuals on the spectrum: "What is so wrong with learning which patterns of relating are more problematic than others in order to organize interaction designed to bring the maximum success more often, and not compound a constant sense of social failure and isolation?" (*Exposure Anxiety* 207).

Andersen's story suggests that the bargain doesn't work, however, and may even be self-destructive. Trading her voice for a pair of legs does not make the prince want to marry her: "He loved her the way that one loves a dear sweet child, but it never occurred to him to make her his queen" (*Stories* 97). The mermaid "wished that she could live among them," but in the end that is proved to be an impossibility, and she dissolves into sea foam, voiceless, formless, alone.

The little mermaid knows her difference sets her apart from people she would like to be friends with. She clearly feels a strong sense of alienation and despair. Andersen repeatedly recorded in his diary that he felt this way as well, and it brought a heavy cloud of depression that plagued him throughout his life.

The Ugly Duckling: A Special, Celebrated Self

Two character traits—otherness and greatness—are combined in many of Andersen's stories, most famously in "The Ugly Duckling" (1844). In these stories, one character is marked out as being *different* from the others. This difference leads to feelings of loneliness and isolation, but as the story progresses it becomes clear that the otherness marks the character as being destined for greatness and good fortune in the end. Andersen consciously wove autobiographical elements into "The Ugly Duckling," telling one critic that the story was "a reflection of my own life" (*Stories* 156). It is easy to trace the parallels between this ugly, awkward, unpopular little swan and Andersen's own childhood experiences. We can see the parallel between his memories of being bullied and the bullying of this creature when a duck bites him and says, "He's so big and strange-looking…It just makes you want to pick on him" (*Stories* 160).

Like the ugly duckling, Andersen had been a quirky boy who was frequently the target of ridicule and rough treatment. Due to his Asperger's Syndrome, he did unusual things, such as knocking on a stranger's door and treating him to a song. Andersen's conversation skills were awkward—he didn't know how to initiate a conversation, how to enter into a normal back and forth exchange, how to consider another's perspective, or how to listen to others. He lectured everyone. He talked incessantly about himself and his own special interests. He sang at inappropriate times. He was gawky and unbelievably clumsy. These are all traits of Asperger's Syndrome that he alluded to in his fairy tales.

Andersen understood that children who were rejected by others could live a very lonely life: "You don't understand me," the duckling says to the other barnyard animals. He sits in a corner, "quite depressed." It is easy to see how the duckling's final triumph in the end, as he fulfills his destiny to become a handsome swan, compares to Andersen's rising literary success, which raised him above his competitors. But the swan does not realize he has had a change of appearance, thus a change of fortune, until he looks into the mirror-like surface of the water to see how he has changed: "what did he see on the clear surface of the water? He saw his own image" (*Stories* 164). His destiny has been fulfilled—he has assumed the role that fate picked out for him at birth. And, once again, the mirror functions as a trope for self-recognition and self-knowledge. The duckling doesn't really become a swan until he peers into the pond and sees that it is so. The character with autism learns the great importance of self-confidence and self-understanding. Andersen was aware of the parallels between himself and his famous duckling character, calling the tale "a *reflection* of my own life" (*Stories* 156, emphasis added).

What I find heartening here is that Andersen, like the Ugly Duckling, did realize he was different, but as he portrayed himself in this fairy tale, his difference made him not only *special*, but *superior* to the others. Being "other," for Andersen, was equivalent to being unique, rare, or chosen. When he reflected upon all the achievements of his life, and remembered how he had worked so hard to overcome various disadvantages, the clouds of depression dispersed and he was a happy, satisfied person. The self-confidence he displayed in the face of his disability was truly amazing.

Use of Symbol

The superficial qualities of Andersen's characters were ideal for the kind of writing he was to become most famous for. The folk wisdom expressed in fairy tales does not rely on psychological or philosophical analysis, but rather on the occult meaning presented by symbol or metaphor. It was Andersen's discovery of the power of symbol that elevated his tales to the status of literary classics.

Not surprisingly, many of the symbols Andersen relies on carry special meaning if viewed in terms of his place on the spectrum. In "The Princess and the Pea," for example, the bruised girl who sleeps atop 20 mattresses has become a universal symbol for the person who is highly sensitive to physical discomfort (individuals with AS are usually tormented by clothing labels, scratchy fabric, tight shoes, and so on). In "The Steadfast Tin Soldier," the hero's oddly-shaped body signifies that he is a misfit, different from the other toy soldiers in the household. Andersen is not the only autistic writer to represent his difference symbolically—Yeats, Dickinson, and Melville also did this.

Many individuals on the spectrum are confused about their identities and wish to understand themselves better—mirrors symbolize the yearning for self-understanding in several Andersen stories, including "The Emperor's New Clothes," "The Red Shoes," "The Ugly Duckling," and "The Snow Queen." Sometimes the mirror is cracked, representing a diffused identity. Andersen's amazing talent for investing these objects with rich symbolic meaning is apparent in the way they have become archetypal symbols that all readers can understand and identify with. Indeed, they have become universally significant in western culture.

The Snow Queen: An Allegory of Autism

The Andersen fairy tale that reveals most about autism, the one that we could rightfully call "an autistic fairy tale," is "The Snow Queen" (1845). This is not to say that Andersen consciously set out to describe his condition, but that he unwittingly created an allegory for a relationship he understood well—between one person who has autism and one person who doesn't. The story, "A Tale in Seven Stories," has much to tell us if we read it as an allegory of autism.

In the beginning of the first story, we are told about a mirror that has special qualities: "it would shrink everything that was good and beautiful to almost nothing, and it would magnify whatever was worthless and ugly and make it seem even worse" (*Stories* 169). The evil mirror can only focus on what is wrong, and never on what is right. The mirror is dropped and falls to earth, shattering into a million splinters. The splinters fly about and are lodged in people's eyes and hearts, changing the victims into negative, disagreeable people.

In other stories, Andersen uses the mirror as a point of "self-reflection" so that the character—the Emperor, the Ugly Duckling, Karen in "The Red Shoes"—can pause for a moment to figure out who he or she really is. But in "The Snow Queen," the hexed mirror serves as a symbol for the self that suffers from depression, anxiety, and anguish. Bits of the mirror are even fashioned into glasses that, when worn, change the wearer's perspective into one that sees only the negative.

The story shifts to the plight of two happy children, Kay and Gerda, who are as close as brother and sister. They love each other and play happily with the roses that grow in the garden. Innocence breeds happiness, and the children are unaware of the darker nature of things in the outside world.

Winter arrives, and with it the cold. But the children can fortify themselves against the cold with the love they show each other, and with the stories that Grandmother tells them. The love keeps them warm, and the stories provide them with meaning. But even love and stories are not enough to keep them safe. The Snow Queen appears at their window, and she is Kay's frosty nemesis:

> The snowflake grew bigger and bigger until, at last, it turned into a woman; she wore the finest white gauze made of millions of star-like flakes. She was delicate and beautiful but made of blinding, glimmering ice. Yet she was alive. Her eyes stared out like two bright stars, but there was no calm or peace in them. She nodded toward the window and waved her hand. The little boy was frightened. (*Stories* 172)

The Queen of Autism has appeared at the window, and she has marked the boy for induction into her kingdom.

Soon after her visit, a splinter from the mirror enters Kay's eye and stings his heart. He isn't the same child after that moment. He criticizes Gerda, argues with Grandma, and takes no pleasure in roses, stories, or other people. Kay becomes a scientist, using a magnifying glass to study the formation of snowflakes. "Look how well designed they are," he comments after noticing their perfect symmetry (*Stories* 174). The flat, 2-D nature of the snowflakes is reminiscent of beautiful paper cutouts that Andersen made to entertain himself. Kay says he now prefers snowflakes to flowers.

Soon after this, the Snow Queen gets her hooks into him and pulls him further away from the warm love of his family. She tows his sled to the north, land of ice and snow. Kay is terrified: "he let go of the rope to get loose from the sleigh, but it didn't do any good. His tiny sled was stuck, and it went as fast as the wind. He shouted very loudly, but no one heard him" (*Stories* 175). When the Snow Queen finally brings him to her castle, he forgets all about Gerda, Grandmother, and home. He is lost to them. Parents who feel they have lost their children to autism would recognize their plight in this scenario. Children with autism often pull away from demonstrations of love and affection. They won't be held. They won't make eye contact. They won't engage in conversation. They are, from the parent's perspective, citizens of another country, living inside another type of reality, one that seems cold and emotionless to observers.

Kay soon demonstrates his abilities in math—he is a savant who can solve tricky math problems in his head, calculate square miles, and extrapolate populations. He doesn't miss Gerda or Grandmother at all.

But Gerda hasn't given up on her beloved brother. She journeys from home and travels far and wide, enduring harsh conditions and suffering from hunger and cold in her search. She refuses to give up. She will find him or she will die trying. Gerda is the neurotypical relative who is desperate to find a cure, or at least an answer. Who won't give up trying, no matter what.

When Gerda arrives at the Snow Queen's castle, she is bewildered and confused by the world she has entered. The Snow Queen sits, emotionless, enthroned on an icy lake that is called "The Mirror of the Mind." Like the mirror mentioned in the story's beginning, this mirror is shattered and cracked into a thousand pieces. The identities of the Queen, Kay, and presumably other victims are also fragmented and unstable.

And what is Kay doing? He is working on a puzzle: *the ice puzzle of the mind*. He is studying "ingenious patterns" in the fractured ice pieces of the Mirror of the Mind. He is moving them around, trying to form the word *eternity*, for she has promised him freedom when he accomplishes this feat. It is an impossible task that the Queen has asked him to do. He is so focused on solving the puzzle that he has stopped feeling the cold, and is turning blue, almost black. The cold might kill him, but still he labors single-mindedly on solving the puzzle in front of him. "Kay was all alone in the big, empty, icy room that was miles long. He looked at the pieces of ice and thought and thought until his head ached" (*Stories* 201). This is a picture of the autistic mind at work. This is a picture of the autistic self fixedly searching for meaning among puzzle pieces that don't fit together. This is a picture of a boy who lives under the power of the Snow Queen.

Can Gerda save him? When she recognizes him, she rushes over and hugs him with joy and relief and love. He sits, stiff and cold, but her warm tears flow and flow until they've melted the splinter in his heart. The chill of autism and the pervasive anxiety and depression that have plagued Kay are gone. The spell is broken and he is free to leave. "Gerda kissed his cheeks, and they turned red; she kissed his eyes, and they shined like hers; she kissed his hands and feet, and he became healthy and fit" (*Stories* 202). The children journey home, and delight to find the roses blooming and Grandmother reading in her rocking chair. The stories will once again bring meaning. The roses will continue to bloom, despite the fact that winter will come again and will continue to be a part of life. Love cannot eliminate autism, but it has saved Kay from the fatal freeze. Kay can bear the cold with a good friend by his side. This ending reflects Andersen's understanding that the warm love of friendship is good medicine for people who are self-involved, distant, and preoccupied with surfaces. When Andersen's dead body was found, a leather pouch containing a letter from a woman he loved was found tied around his neck.

This story has a special resonance for parents of children with autism who have watched in fear and helplessness as their children are inducted into faraway kingdoms. We have felt anguish at recognizing the Snow Queen at the window. We have watched our child working endlessly at puzzles that have no solutions. Our hearts break when a child will not accept our love. Like Gerda, we would travel to any place, no matter how far away, to save our sons and daughters. And we live on the faith that our love for our children will somehow improve their lives.

Conclusion

Andersen was born before the condition of autism had even been identified. Yet he knew, as well as the people around him knew, that there was something about him that was just a little strange. This is a hard thing to admit to oneself, and it is understandable why someone would struggle to explore this issue in an autobiography, which is one reason why he was so challenged by that genre. In a letter to a friend, he once wrote, "I am a peculiar being!… I can never enjoy the present, my life is in the past and in the future, and there is in reality too little for a real man. I have been in bad, very bad spirits" (Andersen, quoted in Fitzgerald *Genesis* 47). In writing his life story over and over again, he was hoping he would eventually figure out who he was.

Fortunately for Andersen, and for the world, he also dipped his pen into the ink to try his hand at writing fairy tales. In this genre, he was able to pin down and confront the feelings that had eluded him in his autobiography. The fairy tales allowed him to explore the nagging feelings of insecurity, loneliness, frustration, anger, and shame that had plagued him throughout his life. By using symbol and allegory instead of direct exposition, he was able to share something of what it felt like to be a man with autism living in the 19th century. But the fairy tales also gave him the opportunity to share his unfailing optimism, his joyful spirit, and his well-deserved pride. His fairy tales enabled him to entertain us with his belief in miracles.

Recognizing that Hans Christian Andersen had Asperger's Syndrome, and recognizing that his stories were influenced by this, gives us the opportunity to learn about the connections between an author's neurological wiring and his way of telling a story: autism not only gave him the materials to write about, but also the persistence, creativity, and intelligence he needed to become a successful author. His status as world-class writer can only be enhanced by the recognition that his stories, postcards from the autistic world, have much to teach us about the "ice puzzles of the mind."

Works Cited

Andersen, Hans Christian. *The Diaries of Hans Christian Andersen*. Selected and translated by Patricia L. Conroy and Sven H. Rossel. Seattle: University of Washington Press, 1990.

---. *The Fairy Tale of My Life*. Originally published by London: Paddington Press, Ltd., 1871. Re-published by New York: Cooper Square Press, 2000.

---. *The Stories of Hans Christian Andersen*. Translated by Diana Crone Frank and Jeffrey Frank. Durham: Duke University Press, 2005.

---. *The True Story of My Life*. 1847. http://www.onlineliterature.com/hans_christian_andersen.

Andersen, Jens. *Hans Christian Andersen: A New Life*. New York: Duckworth, 2005.

Fitzgerald, Michael. *Autism and Creativity*. New York: Routledge, 2004.

---. *The Genesis of Artistic Creativity: Asperger's Syndrome and the Arts*. London: Jessica Kingsley Publishers, 2005.

Sacks, Oliver. "Foreword." Temple Grandin's *Thinking in Pictures*. New York: Vintage, 1995.

Williams, Donna. *Autism and Sensing: The Unlost Instinct*. London: Jessica Kingsley Publishers, 1998.

---. *Exposure Anxiety: The Invisible Cage*. London: Jessica Kingsley Publishers, 2003.

Wing, Lorna. *The Autistic Spectrum: A Parents' Guide to Understanding and Helping Your Child*. Berkeley: Ulysses Press, 2001.

Wullschlager, Jackie. *Hans Christian Andersen: The Life of a Storyteller*. New York: Penguin, 2000.

CHAPTER THREE

Henry David Thoreau

Thoreau and Asperger's Syndrome

Henry David Thoreau (1817–1862) occupies a central place in American literature. He never wrote a novel or a short story, and his poetry is mediocre at best, but his journals, speeches, and essays are presented as classic literature in anthologies and college courses around the world. *Walden* (1854), which chronicles his two-year sojourn in a cabin in the woods, is justifiably considered a literary masterpiece in terms of its style and its message. In *Walden*, Thoreau celebrates the American values of self-reliance, pragmatism, and above all, individualism.

Thoreau was a quirky man. He demonstrated so many traits of Asperger's Syndrome (AS) that it seems very likely he was affected by it. His social skills and language abilities were undeniably impaired—he was isolated, socially awkward, and a poor conversationalist. He lectured others on his special subjects, spoke with a slight impediment, and had difficulty making eye contact with others. Cognitively, he was an extremely intelligent man whose investigations into the natural history of Massachusetts are precise and thorough. Like most people on the spectrum, he tended to perseverate on beloved topics—in Thoreau's case, his special interest was Walden Pond and the flora and fauna that surrounded it. Although he was hyper-lexic, he was a terrible speller. And although his handwriting was poor, he was a brilliant writer. His style was highly detailed, self-reflexive, and complex: Asperger's Syndrome no doubt played a strong role in shaping his distinctive writing style, as well as determining its unusual content. It also answers questions about his motives for writing both *Walden* (a philosophical memoir about his two-year stay in the woods) and the political essay "Civil Disobedience."

Asperger Syndrome's Influence: Reliance on Visual Details

Temple Grandin, a noted author with autism, explains that her thinking style differs from that of most neurotypicals in that she thinks in pictures, not in words. Her experiences with perception, analysis, and memory are all based on specific visual images and details that she can store and retrieve at will: "I think in pictures," she writes. "Words are like a second language to me. I translate both spoken and written words into full-color movies, complete with sound, which run like a VCR tape in my head" (*Thinking* 19).

Thoreau, too, was a highly visual person. For one thing, his sense of sight was acute. He could see a tiny bird at a great distance, and not only identify which type of bird it was, but even which specific bird. Fitzgerald notes that "persons with autism have strengths in the visuo-spatial area" because they are usually right-hemisphere dominant. The right hemisphere "thinks visually in pictures and images" (*Genesis* 203). We see this visual emphasis reflected in Thoreau's writing style. *Walden* is constructed with a scaffolding of detail: he takes the time to describe specific lakes, stones, trees, plants, birds, animals, clouds, fish, insects, ice formations, and so on. He loves nature and finds beauty in the tiniest ant or flower or bean. In his journal he recognizes this tendency: "I see details, not wholes nor the shadow of the whole" (*A Year* 167). The tendency to focus on brush strokes rather than the whole canvas is common among people with AS. Fitzgerald refers to this as the "Asperger type of approach" (203).

Thoreau's *Walden* is a catalogue of different types of details. In each chapter he seems to favor one kind of detail and uses it over and over to make his point:

- In "Economy" he provides numbers for all aspects of his life—he records every penny he earned over a two-year period, as well as every cent he spent on building his house, on food, and on his household expenses.
- "The Ponds" is filled with beautiful visual imagery that describes not only Walden Pond but other ponds in the vicinity. The chapter is filled with many color words to capture the color of the water as it changes throughout the day or year: yellowish, yellow, green, green as grass, light green, uniform dark green, vivid green, vitreous greenish blue, blue, pure water blue, sky blue, darker blue, light blue, cerulean, dark slate-color, black, brown, colorless.
- "Winter Animals" lists dozens of species of animals and reads like a field guide for fauna common to New England: foxes, dogs, red squirrels, rabbits, deer, mice, hares, skunks, bears, wildcats, and so on.
- "Spring" contains a long list of dates as Thoreau remembers back to the annual freezing and thawing of ice through the years (the winter of 1852–1853 was an especially severe winter).
- Although most of his details are visual, in "Sounds" he lists examples of all kinds of noises: birdsong, wind, train whistle, bell, blue jay, fox, squirrel, spinning wheel, butter churn, and kettle (to mention just a few)—and he enjoys such onomatopoetic words as *bark, hum, buzz, cluck, whip-poor-will,* the *hoo hoo hoo* of an owl, and the *t-r-r-r-o-o-n-k*! of a frog's morning song.

This technique of cataloguing details is used by other AS writers as well: Herman Melville, Lewis Carroll, Opal Whiteley, and James Joyce have all developed their writing this way at times. Thoreau confessed in his journal that he feared he was becoming overly fixated on detail at the expense of the big picture: "I fear that the character of my knowledge is from year to year becoming more distinct and scientific; that, in exchange for views as wide as heaven's cope, I am being narrowed down to the field of the microscope" (*A Year* 167). The details do give us pictures and sounds to help render the scenes, but Thoreau is perhaps less successful at weaving them together into an overall story. The reader feels bogged down after a while by the long lists and wonders where Thoreau is going. This process of accumulating details is somewhat similar to the way children with autism play with a toy such as Legos: they arrange the Legos in long lines organized by color or size, but they do not integrate all of the pieces into a pre-designed vehicle or building.

The Movement toward Meaning: from Concrete to Abstract

If Thoreau had had classic autism, he might not have had the central coherence necessary to integrate the details into an overall meaning, but since his form of ASD was Asperger's Syndrome, he did want the reader to understand his message on a deeper level than mere physical imagery. He did so, in *Walden*, by moving from image to metaphor, and from metaphor to universal theme. He worked from small to big. Curiously, this parallels the way one autistic savant draftsman worked (as observed by Laurent Mottron): first he started with a small, unimportant detail, then he expanded that into an entire drawing of a project (Fitzgerald 203). Most draftsmen would start with a larger concept of a draft, then work toward detail later.

Grandin believes that neurotypical thought process moves from abstract to concrete, from general to specific: first comes the idea, then the example. "Many [neurotypical] people see a generalized generic church rather than specific churches and steeples when they hear or read the word 'steeple.' Their thought patterns move from a general concept to specific examples" (27). But for her, and for many others on the autistic spectrum, the reverse is true: "Unlike those of most [neurotypical] people, my thoughts move from video-like, specific images to generalizations and concepts" (28). Thoreau made a similar observation about his own thought process: he recognized that his writing pattern consisted of "bringing the little into the large" (Harding 454). In other words, Thoreau started with a tiny detail and expanded that detail into a metaphor, finally teasing the metaphor into a larger theme.

In the chapter of *Walden* called "Reading," for example, Thoreau first makes a statement that provides a specific, visual image: "I kept Homer's Iliad on my table" (80). A few sentences later, he expands that image into a more general statement: "The student may read Homer or Aeschylus in the Greek without danger of dissipation or luxuriousness" (80). Further on, he expands the statement into a philosophical concept: "To read well, that is, to read true books in a true spirit, is a noble exercise, and one that will task the reader more than any exercise which the customs of the day esteem" (81).

Another example of this pattern appears in the chapter called "Sounds." First comes the specific detail: "The Fitchburg Railroad touches the pond about a hundred rods south of where I dwell" (91). Next comes the metaphor, comparing a train to some kind of great mythological beast: "When I hear the iron horse make the hills echo with his snort-like thunder, shaking the earth with his feet... it seems as if the earth had got a race now worthy to inhabit it" (91). Finally, his prose moves to the universal concept, in this case arguing that the railroad riding on its tracks functions as a symbol for individual destiny: "Every path but your own is the path of fate. Keep on your own track, then" (93).

Focus on the Self

Walden is hard to categorize. It is at once a natural history of one specific geographical region, a transcendental call-to-arms, and it is also, oddly, a very personal diary. No matter what purported topic Thoreau chose to write about, he ended up ultimately writing about himself. This is common among AS writers, as Fitzgerald observes: "Literary works by persons with Asperger's Syndrome often have strong autobiographical elements (e.g. Conan Doyle and Sherlock Holmes). They are thus a form of self-expression for persons with Asperger's Syndrome, who find other forms of expression difficult" (239). It is hard to say whether Thoreau focused so much on himself because he was overly egotistical or because he lacked self-esteem. It is clear that he enjoyed writing about himself and that it gave him pleasure. The opening two paragraphs of *Walden* use the personal pronoun "I" 18 times. He openly acknowledged this mirror-gazing: "I should not talk so much about myself if there were anybody else whom I knew as well" (15). In his private journal, he noted that he thought every author revealed things about himself through his writings: "The author's character is read from title-page to end" (*Writer's Journal* 4). Thus it is with *Walden*—he invites us to look into the pond with him, but what we find there is his reflected face. If we read *Walden* with the understanding that Thoreau had Asperger's Syndrome, it becomes clear that his place on the spectrum is the driving force behind most of the philosophical conclusions that he reaches.

Walden and the Asperger Lifestyle

Readers who are not aware of Thoreau's place on the autistic spectrum might read *Walden* as a guide to living a simple but richly rewarding life. And that it surely is. But taking a closer look at some of Thoreau's principles—and studying them within the context of how Asperger's Syndrome shapes preferences and habits—gives us a valuable glimpse into an AS man's attempt to understand—and defend—himself and his behaviors. As such, the text becomes something of a guidebook that could easily find a place on the shelf beside other autism "self-help" books. His mandates are few but they are clearly outlined.

1. Preserve a sameness of environment and a compulsive adherence to routines

Anyone who has read *Walden* will surely remember the position Thoreau takes on clothing. From a philosophical perspective, he argues (for five pages) that human beings should not become overly preoccupied with fashion or variety where clothing is concerned. "Perhaps," he argues, "we are led oftener by the love of novelty and a regard for the opinions of men, in procuring [clothing], than by a true utility" (27). Of course his point is a good one—too many of us spend too much money and time on wardrobes that are merely put together to impress the people we encounter. But as an individual with Asperger's Syndrome, Thoreau is also defending his preference for wearing the same comfy outfit day after day, no matter how dirty or unfashionable it may be. People with fancy, uncomfortable wardrobes "cannot know the comfort of wearing a suit that fits," he argues, since it is only by wearing the same outfit day after day that it takes on the "impress" of one's body (27). This sentiment is surely shared by the leagues of AS teenaged boys who wear the same comfortable t-shirt, sweat pants, and slip-on shoes to school each day, despite the fact that their neurotypical sisters have closets bursting with the latest uncomfortable fashions. As a young man, Thoreau customized his outfit to make it even more useful, albeit peculiar: he marked inches on his walking stick that it might be used to measure things he encountered on his walks, and fixed a special "specimen box" inside his hat to safely stow any found object that he wished to carry with him.

Thoreau's position on food is similar. He writes that ideally each person should grow his own food, should eat it raw or lightly cooked, and should have a simple and unvaried diet. He eschews food that is exotic, fancy, or rich, preferring instead a basic meal of rice, carrots, beans, and potatoes. For two years, Thoreau's diet consisted of only eight or nine different things, and only water to drink. Thoreau recommends this course for others, as well:

> If one would live simply and eat only the crop which he raised, and raise no more than he ate, and not exchange it for an insufficient quantity of more luxurious and expensive things, he would need to cultivate only a few rods of ground, and... it would be cheaper to spade up that than to use oxen to plow it. (50)

In other words, eating simple foods is responsible, practical, and healthy. One suspects, however, that Thoreau simply *preferred* the taste and texture of simple grains and vegetables, as many AS people do. A plate of plain white rice and carrot sticks will keep most AS boys happier than a plate of *Coq au Vin* ever could. Thoreau can defend his finicky palate and take the moral high road at the same time. Even better that his food of choice has an intellectual association: "It was fit that I should live on rice, mainly, who loved so well the philosophy of India" (54).

As for shelter, when he is not outdoors Thoreau prefers small, enclosed spaces. He spends much of his adult life living at home with his parents, passing most of his time in his upstairs attic bedroom, reading, writing, and studying his nature specimens (he had over 1000 pressed plants). Not surprisingly, when he builds his cabin near Walden Pond he deliberately makes it small and cozy: 10 feet by 15, with a small cellar for storing roots and vegetables. This turns out to be the ideal size for a simple cot, a writing desk, a small stove, and a fireplace. The essence of his preference for small spaces is evident in his wistful yearning to live in a coffin-like wooden box:

> I used to see a large box by the railroad, six feet long by three wide, in which the laborers locked up their tools at night; and it suggested to me that every man who was hard pushed might get such a one for a dollar, and, having bored a few auger holes in it, to admit the air at least, get into it when it rained and at night, and hook down the lid and so have freedom in his love and in his soul be free... You could sit up as late as

> you pleased, and, whenever you got up, go abroad without any landlord or houselord dogging you for rent... I am far from jesting. (32)

Thoreau preaches against the sin of building a large, ostentatious house. He rants against middle-class dwellings that inevitably become cluttered by excess: too much furniture, art, draperies, and so on. Such houses, he argues, become prisons, as we must spend half of our time earning the mortgage payment and the other half maintaining our investment. He is right to argue against frivolous excesses that tax the environment and burden the soul. But once again, the writing seems to be based on Asperger preferences rather than philosophical principles.

Thoreau writes about how his choices in clothing, food, and shelter reflect his philosophy in life. "An individual's first duty is to live his life as his principles demand," he maintains. He presents careful arguments for choosing the simple over the complex, the home-made over the manufactured, the humble over the grand, and for preferring consistency rather than variety. His choices seem to reflect his interest in eastern philosophy and give him a somewhat ascetic air. But I would argue that his writing also vindicates the lifestyle choices he has made for himself. His preferences are rooted in his place on the autism spectrum.

2. Pursue all-absorbing narrow interests exclusively and repetitively

People with Asperger's Syndrome are usually known to have a "special interest" that absorbs much of their time and attention. Everyone seems to know such a child who is obsessed by either dinosaurs or trains to the extent that he can recite every available fact on the topic and will do so, with pleasure, whether the listener is interested or not. Thoreau's special interest was his pond: Walden became his home, his school, his worksite, and his church. One of the first memories he writes about is his mother taking him to

Walden's shores for a picnic when he was a small boy. He built his first boat at age 16 in order to study the pond more intimately:

> I have spent many an hour, when I was younger, floating over its surface as the zephyr willed, having paddled my boat to the middle, and lying on my back across the seats, in a summer forenoon, dreaming awake, until I was aroused by the boat touching the sand, and I arose to see what shore my fates had impelled me to. (142)

As a man he builds his first home on the very shore of the pond, using its stones for his fireplace and its sand for mortar. He eats its fish, drinks its water, and taps it to irrigate his beans.

In the chapter called "The Ponds," he gives a good basic description of Walden: "It is a clear and deep green well, half a mile long and a mile and three quarters in circumference, and contains about sixty-one and a half acres; a perennial spring in the midst of pine and oak woods, without any visible inlet or outlet except by the clouds and evaporation" (131). Whereas some of Thoreau's writings are philosophical and didactic, when he writes about the pond his writing reaches a sustained level of detail like a new mother describing her first-born child. He discusses the clarity of the water, how far one can see into it, and what fabulous ice it makes. He shares his observations of the water's depth and how it changes from season to season, and from year to year (in the summer of 1852 it was five feet higher than in 1845). He puzzles over how the pond got its name. He catalogues every fish that swims in the water, every bird that flies over it, and every animal that drinks from its shores. He composes metaphors to represent the lake poetically (it is the earth's eye). And on and on he goes.

Years after he finished writing *Walden*, Thoreau continued to record his observations of the plants that grew around the pond and in the neighboring woods. He filled countless pages in a journal of his findings, and prepared notes for a book-length compilation of native plant life. Like many people with AS he was an expert researcher, feverishly reading books from the Boston Society of Natural History (he climbed in the window some mornings so he could start reading before the janitor unlocked the door) as well as from Harvard University and from Emerson's private library. Unfortunately, tuberculosis took him away before he could finish this project. Today, naturalists still use his work to understand how plant life has been diminishing recently due to the changes in climate. Sadly, his lists are now becoming elegies for the many plants that no longer grow in the wilds of Massachusetts.

Like Yeats, Thoreau composed his writings in his head while he walked, and merely committed them to paper when he sat at his desk (Stevenson 16). A humorous example of Thoreau's single-minded ability to pursue his interests occurred once when he was walking on a trail through the woods of Massachusetts. He had consulted his compass and determined to walk in one direction only for that day. When he happened upon a farmhouse on his path, he did not detour, but opened the front door, strode on through the house, and went out the back door, "leaving the astonished farmer and his family speechless around their dining table" (Harding 295).

Part of Thoreau's genius surely lies in his ability to observe, understand, and document the natural world around him. Yet he brings his own special kind of genius to the project by translating the world around him into a prayer book for humanity. In *Walden,* Thoreau transforms natural objects into transcendent symbols that beg us to contemplate the divine messages all around us.

An example: curious to know which exact place in the pond is the deepest, Thoreau brings his surveying skills to bear and relentlessly maps and measures his pond. The deepest place, he observes, at exactly "one hundred and two feet," is located at the intersection between two lines—the one that marks the widest part of the pond, and the one that marks the longest. This fact interests Thoreau and he meditates upon it for several pages until he draws out a message for us all:

> What I have observed of the pond is no less true in ethics. It is the law of average. Such a rule of the two diameters not only guides us toward the sun in the system and the heart in man, but draw lines through the length and breadth of the aggregate of a man's particular daily behaviors and waves of life into his coves and inlets, and where they intersect will be the height or depth of his character. (207)

In other words, we can measure our lives in the same way he measured the pond, and in doing so come to find and understand our true center and our deepest places. Understanding the pond helps us understand ourselves.

Thoreau understands that nurturing his special interest makes him feel comfortable and happy. We can almost imagine him hugging himself as he muses "I love to weigh, to settle, to gravitate toward that which most strongly and rightfully attracts me" (233). His obsession with observing and cataloguing the natural world in his back yard means more to him than anything, which is perhaps why he remains an under-employed, solitary bachelor in the woods. He can't allow anything to come between him and his quest for learning more about nature. He is not just posturing when he states: "Rather than love, than money, than fame, give me truth" (233).

Of course he also recognizes that other people can and should follow their own inclinations and interests. He gives his blessing to others with instructions to find their own Walden Pond in a passage that is one of the most quoted from Thoreau: "I learned this, at least, by my experiment: that if one advances confidently in the direction of his dreams, and endeavors to live the life which he has imagined, he will meet with a success unexpected in common hours" (228). This is an optimistic encouragement for others with autism and Asperger's Syndrome to continue following their own special interests, even if they run counter to society. Thoreau's willingness to move closer to his beloved pond for two years in order to study it more closely, through all seasons, around all hours of the clock, gives him the chance to nurture his special interest as well as the inspiration and devotion necessary to create one of the greatest works of American literature.

3. Restrict social interaction and arrange for solitude

As stated previously, when Thoreau was with others his social skills were awkward, yet strangely when he was in a group he preferred the spotlight, wanted to share his knowledge, and wanted to talk more than listen. He made many social blunders and could not sustain polite conversation for long—asking personal questions or listening to other people's small talk bored him exceedingly. Over time he seemed to realize that he was different from other men his age, but I'm sure he never dreamed that one factor related to this difference was his neurological wiring. Instead, his writings make it clear that he felt others were not *worthy* of his company, and that he preferred his own company to anyone else's because he simply found himself to be more *interesting*.

It's hard to tell whether he's being serious or ironic when he shares what it's like for him to walk through the village of Concord. He describes the two sides of the street, each lined with shops and businesses and houses, and compares walking through the town to running the gauntlet. To walk through a community is to be assaulted on all sides by people who want to talk, chat, and visit with him. For one thing, there might be attractive young females lurking about. Even worse, there might be gossipy older women to contend with. But Thoreau has an exit strategy: "For the most part I escaped wonderfully from these dangers, either by proceeding at once boldly and without deliberation to the goal, as is recommended by those who run the gauntlet, or by keeping my thoughts on high things... Sometimes I bolted suddenly, and nobody could tell my whereabouts" (126). An AS teenager facing his first day of middle school could surely relate to this metaphor.

Many people with AS harbor the dream of living in a tiny house, all alone, in the middle of the woods. But Thoreau actually made his dream come true and lived to tell the tale (as did Sherwood

Anderson). What he finds there is a deep peace that begins at the break of day: "I sat in my sunny doorway from sunrise till noon, rapt in a revery, amidst the pines and hickories and sumachs, in undisturbed solitude and stillness, while the birds sang around or flitted noiseless through the house..." (88). He continues on till sunset, after the last train whistle has died down: "now that the cars are gone by and all the restless world with them and the fishes in the pond no longer feel their rumbling, I am more alone than ever" (96). He feels calm and relaxed when alone.

He maintains that solitude is good for his mental health, and defends his choice vigorously. "I find it wholesome," he writes, "to be alone the greater part of the time. To be in company, even with the best, is soon wearisome and dissipating. I love to be alone. I never found the companion that was so companionable as solitude" (104). Fortunately for him, he likes himself and enjoys spending time with his own thoughts and solo experiences. He doesn't require company or entertainment, because "my life itself was become my amusement and never ceased to be novel" (89).

Thoreau argues that self-reliance, a natural consequence of being alone much of the time, is more noble than depending on others. Charity is abominable, to Thoreau's way of thinking, and he refuses to give or receive it. In fact, he claims that if someone knocked on his door offering to help in some way, he would run in the other direction. His emphasis on a Yankee do-it-yourself attitude is in many ways refreshing and hopeful: "I know of no more encouraging fact than the unquestionable ability of man to elevate his life by a conscious endeavor" (74). And yet, his complete inability to empathize with the poor or down-trodden seems to be a serious character flaw.

Doing projects without help is a good way to feel proud of yourself, and spending time away from others is a good way to nurture your ego. After bragging about how cheaply he was able to build his own house, Thoreau celebrates his egotism in this way: "If I seem to boast more than is becoming, my excuse is that I brag for humanity rather than for myself; and my shortcomings and inconsistencies [i.e. borrowed land, borrowed tools, free wood, sand, and stone] do not affect the truth of my statement" (46).

Independence is freedom. This means not taking on any commitments to other people or institutions. "As long as possible live free and uncommitted," he advises; "it makes but little difference whether you are committed to a farm or the county jail" (69). Not only should you avoid commitment, but you should not be dependent on help from others, either. Thoreau's egotism convinces him that his little dependencies, however, "don't count." It's easy to spot his hypocrisy. He borrows an axe, but returns it "sharper than I received it" (40). He cuts down some of Emerson's trees, but because he appreciates the trees so much he feels "more the friend than the foe of the pine tree" (41). He must ask a few friends to help him raise his rafters, but maintains that he does this to foster a feeling of "neighborliness" rather than because he really needs their help. He is able to convince us, and himself, that he is a completely independent person, despite the fact that any high school reader could tell you that he was squatting on someone else's land while living at Walden Pond. Like many people on the autistic spectrum, the truth is he was never able to live completely independently—he lived with his parents, with the Emerson family, or on land that Emerson let him borrow.

Many people with Asperger's Syndrome live alone because their nervous system can't handle the "overload" of being with others all the time. Some live alone because they can't find a partner to share a life or lifestyle with. Lewis Carroll and Hans Christian Andersen were confirmed bachelors. Yeats didn't marry until he was in his fifties. Sherwood Anderson married four different wives, including one who lived in a separate house from him. Emily Dickinson and Opal Whiteley both loved several men but did not live with them or marry. Thoreau champions *his* preference for living alone by claiming that it stems from his noble philosophy of self-reliance. At the end of his life, however, as he lay in his parents' home dying of tuberculosis, Thoreau's heart softened toward other people as good wishes poured in from around the world. According to his sister

Sophia, "He was greatly moved by the attentions of his friends and neighbors. He came to feel very differently toward people and said if he had known [how much people cared] he wouldn't have been so offish" (Harding 462).

4. Develop your identity through oppositional behavior

These words of Thoreau would make a great banner in a special needs classroom:

"I was not born to be forced. I will breathe after my own fashion" ("Civil Disobedience" 248). Or, to put this another way, "I'm different—deal with it." If ever a man marched to a different drummer, surely that man would be Henry David Thoreau. In *Walden*, and in countless other pieces of writing, Thoreau exults in his Asperger oppositional behavior and delights in going against the grain. He was, in the words of Robert Louis Stevenson, a "born dissenter" (2).

In *Walden*, Thoreau asserts himself by rebelling against social norms. Instead of living with a family, he lives alone. Instead of living in a village, he lives in the country. Instead of working at a job, he practices subsistence agriculture. He does not attend church. He does not volunteer for social causes. He deliberately wears old, patched clothes, and would rather walk than take a carriage or train. A quick look through the text reveals numerous "pronouncements" on going through life his own way. A few examples:

- "In most books, the I, or first person, is omitted; in this it will be retained" (15).
- "Beware of all enterprises that require new clothes" (29).
- "I would rather sit on a pumpkin and have it all to myself than be crowded on a velvet cushion" (38).
- "What old people say you cannot do, you try and find that you can" (19).

- "If a man does not keep pace with his companions, perhaps it is because he hears a different drummer" (230).
- "Philanthropy is...greatly overrated" (64).

Thoreau comes across as a real curmudgeon in *Walden*: cranky, anti-social, and difficult. Yet he is still loved by a circle of friends and family who recognize and appreciate his good qualities. In *Walden* the oppositional stance reads as a manifesto for romantic individualism, a kind of adolescent rebel yell for going your own way and doing your own thing. But read in the context of Asperger's Syndrome, we can recognize the attempts of a man with autism to claim his own identity by contrasting himself with others. Non-conformist behavior is *very* common among people on the spectrum.

By the time that Thoreau writes "Civil Disobedience" he has polished his rough philosophy into a sparkling gem. This time, there is a purpose to the stubborn contrariness. This time, Thoreau can claim a noble motivation for breaking the rules and going against the norm. His oppositional stubbornness draws attention to a moral purpose, and Thoreau justly becomes a hero to people around the world as a result.

"Civil Disobedience," written in 1848, is an essay that describes how and why Thoreau spent a night in jail in defense of his principles. It was the time of slavery in the United States, and because of this Thoreau refused to pay his taxes. He argued that paying taxes was akin to endorsing the government's spending of that money to uphold the institution of slavery. Rather than support slavery, he made a statement by not paying his tax, and willingly paid the consequence of being incarcerated. It was a personal decision he made in order to take a stand on behalf of his fellow human beings. He did not mind staying the night in jail, and wondered why others who felt the same way about slavery were not in jail beside him.

Compare the pronouncements above, from *Walden*, with these from "Civil Disobedience":

- "That government is best which governs not at all" (236).
- "I think that we should be men first, and subjects afterward" (237).
- "The only obligation which I have a right to assume is to do at any time what I think right" (237).
- "The mass of men serve the State thus, not as men mainly, but as machines, with their bodies" (238).
- "Even voting *for the right* is *doing* nothing for it" (240).
- "If [the law] is of such a nature that it requires you to be the agent of injustice to another, then, I say, break the law" (243).

This time, his contrariness has a very specific focus. This time, his oppositional thinking has a worthy motive and a very noble agenda: slavery is wrong and must be abolished.

Thoreau didn't set out to become famous for spending a night in jail. He merely acted from his conscience and his principles. But in this small action he revealed himself to be a genius in the art of non-violent protest. People heard about his actions. The story was repeated around the world, and his actions played a role in abolishing slavery. Gandhi was inspired by Thoreau, and used his method of non-violent protest to help India win its freedom from England. Martin Luther King was also inspired by Thoreau, and used his method to help Blacks gain Civil Rights in America in the 1960s. The world is surely a better place for us all because of Thoreau and his willingness to stand up for his beliefs. Sometimes it takes a different kind of thinker to create a new and improved way to solve an ongoing, destructive problem.

Coping with Stress: Writing Process as Self-Help

Educators Alan Sohn and Cathy Grayson have studied the connection between stress and behavior in children and teenagers on the spectrum. Their findings reveal that most people with Asperger's Syndrome are living at a high level of anxiety much of the time. Sensory overload, baffling social rules, unpredictable events, and the inability to understand other people can lead to a very high stress level. Just as Thoreau was moving to Walden, he was facing a massive amount of stress: his romantic relationship with Ellen Sewall had failed; his beloved brother John had just died of lockjaw; he was finished with college, but unsure of what to do next; he was feeling society's pressure to find a job and settle down.

When the Asperger individual's stress level reaches an unmanageably high level, according to Sohn and Grayson, certain behaviors often surface. *Walden* is a catalogue of how Thoreau engaged in each of these behaviors as a way of coping with his anxiety:

- having a narrow range of interests, and becoming fixated on certain topics and/or routines (Walden Pond, nature, reading, writing)
- insisting on having things and/or events occur in a certain way (he built his house how he wanted it; scheduled each day as he wished)
- creating their own set of rules for doing something (he did everything himself and did not ask for help)
- preferring to do the same things over and over (get up, swim, eat, work, walk, sleep)
- eating a narrow range of foods (carrots, rice, beans, potatoes)
- intensely disliking loud noises and crowds (he chose the silence of the woods)
- tending to conserve energy and put forth the least effort they can, except with highly preferred activities (at Walden he *only* engaged in highly preferred activities).

Thoreau's self-awareness was incomplete. He knew he "needed" to do certain things, but he didn't quite realize that he needed to do these things in order to assuage the anxiety that besieged him whenever he adopted a neurotypical, "normal" lifestyle. All he knew was that this kind of lifestyle suited him best. And this is why he wrote *Walden*.

Thoreau moved to Walden to escape from the pressures of his life that he found hard to manage because of his Asperger's Syndrome. He wrote his great masterpiece, *Walden,* in order to better understand himself and his peculiar place in the world. The process of writing was therapeutic for him. It allowed him to catalogue the observations and details that were comforting to him. It allowed him to study those details for the metaphorical meaning they could offer. It allowed him to draw from these metaphors a philosophical framework that is bright, noble, worthy, and even enviable. In the end, he created a masterpiece that can be read, at least on one level, as one AS man's journey to understanding not only why, but *how* he marched to the quirky beat of his own drum.

Works Cited

Fitzgerald, Michael. *The Genesis of Autistic Creativity.* London: Jessica Kingsley Publishers, 2005.

Grandin, Temple. *Thinking in Pictures and Other Reports from My Life with Autism.* New York: Vintage, 1996.

Harding, Walter. *The Days of Henry Thoreau.* New York: Knopf, 1965.

Sohn, Alan, and Grayson, Cathy. *Parenting Your Asperger Child: Individualized Solutions for Teaching Your Child Practical Skills.* New York: Perigree Books, 2005.

Stevenson, Robert Louis. "Henry David Thoreau: His Character and Opinions." *Cornhill Magazine* June 1880. http://thoreau.eserver.org/stevens1.html.

Thoreau, Henry David. *Letters to Various Persons.* Boston: Ticknor and Fields, 1865.

---. *Walden and On the Duty of Civil Disobedience.* New York: Collier Books, 1962. All quotations from *Walden* and "Civil Disobedience" are taken from this edition.

CHAPTER FOUR

Herman Melville

Herman Melville, American Genius

Although Herman Melville (1819–1891) never received sufficient recognition for literary genius during his lifetime, he has since come to be known as one of the great patriarchs of American literature. His major works include several novels of life at sea, including *Typee* and *Omoo*, as well as the great psychological novel, *Moby Dick*. During his writing tenure the new "short story" emerged as a legitimate genre, and his stories, including "Bartleby the Scrivener," appeared alongside those of Edgar Allan Poe and Nathaniel Hawthorne as pioneers of a brand new form. "Bartleby" shows the influence of Asperger's Syndrome (AS) in its plot, setting, and characterization. It is also a good example of a short story that reveals how its author understood his own neurological difference and its impact on his work life and family life.

Melville and Asperger's Syndrome

Throughout his life, Melville displayed traits of Asperger's Syndrome. As a boy, young Herman was "backward in speech" (Arvin 17) and "inarticulate" (Robertson-Lorant 25), even though he was highly intelligent. As a teenager, he was withdrawn and usually preferred to be alone. Even as an adult, his social skills remained awkward and he felt uncomfortable around people. Acquaintances remarked that his social skills were hampered by his inability to make "normal" eye contact with others.

He was dark and handsome and he let his hair grow long and wild. He attacked his food at mealtimes like a hungry dog racing to finish the last bone (Delbanco 35), and usually talked with his mouth full. His personal grooming habits and manners were less than stellar, a trait typical of AS males (more than one person remarked that he was not inclined to change his undergarments). Despite the fact that his parents provided him with dancing lessons as a child, he remained clumsy throughout his life. The only place where he became coordinated and graceful was on a ship at sea. He wrote several novels about his adventures as a boat hand, including his most famous, *Moby Dick*.

He had several acquaintances with whom he liked to spend time, but wasn't close to any of them. Aside from perhaps Nathaniel Hawthorne, "none of his friends felt they really knew him" (Delbanco 136). Melville married Elizabeth Shaw and together they had four children. At home, he liked following a rigid schedule of activities for the day, and became angry if his family did not stick to the regime (it was a big problem if his oatmeal or coffee was not prepared the way he liked it). Throughout much of his adult life, he supported himself and his family by writing.

Melville was seen as a study in contrasts: he was both absent-minded and picky, both enigmatic and blunt, both violent and extremely sensitive. Michael Fitzgerald, noting that "no American writer has been more puzzled over," believes that "[Melville's] enigmatic behavior can be ascribed at least in part to Asperger's Syndrome" (50). This assessment not only helps us to understand Melville better, but it also helps us to understand his writing.

A Puzzling Short Story: "Bartleby the Scrivener"

"Bartleby the Scrivener: A Story of Wall Street" is Melville's most famous, and most intriguing, short story. It was published in 1853 in *Putnam's Magazine* over a period of three months. The short story (which is actually a rather long story of 68 pages) tells the story of an older, conservative attorney who employs four people in his Wall Street office. One of them is Bartleby, a young man whose job it is to copy documents all day long, a sort of human Xerox machine. The attorney is initially impressed by Bartleby's neat handwriting, punctuality, and good work habits, even though Bartleby does seem a bit *strange*. He never mixes with his co-workers. He doesn't share meals with anyone. He apparently has no social life. And then, at one point, when the attorney asks Bartleby to help check over his work, he responds with a courteous "I would prefer not to." The lawyer and the others are baffled.

Nobody knows how to respond to Bartleby's polite expression of preferring not to work. The lawyer repeats that request, and others, and Bartleby continues to respond with "I would prefer not to." The lawyer begs him, orders him, bribes him, and wheedles him, and still Bartleby responds with "I would prefer not to." After the lawyer fires him, Bartleby still does not leave the office, giving the lawyer no choice but to vacate the premises himself and move his office elsewhere. At the end of the story the lawyer hears that Bartleby has been hauled away into prison. The lawyer visits him, but in the end Bartleby dies, all alone, in his cell.

This plot is fairly traditional in its presentation of a conflict (Bartleby vs. Lawyer) that escalates as it moves toward a climax (Bartleby hauled away to prison) and final *denouement* (Bartleby dies). Yet it is possible to see traces of an AS type of storytelling nonetheless. For one thing, we find the use of *repetition* in this story as we do in many stories by AS writers. The lawyer asks Bartleby to do something; Bartleby says he prefers not to. This pattern is repeated more than 20 times in the story. It is surely a perseverative plot feature.

Another AS storytelling feature is the quality of *randomness* that the reader is confronted with. Bartleby just shows up one day looking for work. We don't know where he lives, who his family is, or what kind of life he's had so far. At first Bartleby works hard for his boss, but inexplicably he stops one day, without any explanation. The lawyer and co-workers never get a justification for why Bartleby won't do his assigned tasks. It seems very arbitrary to them and to the reader. We understand that the story's ending—the death of Bartleby—follows as a consequence of his refusal to cooperate with authority. But are we sure about that? One student of mine said she thought Bartleby had some kind of terminal illness, such as cancer, and that he didn't feel well in the story. That was a good guess, but since we never learn for sure why he fails to cooperate, the ending still feels arbitrary.

An Autistic Setting

Most of the story is set inside the lawyer's office. Melville gives the reader plenty of details to be able to visualize the entire setup. The office is located on Wall Street on the upper floor of a solid, brick building. Bartleby is given a desk close to the desk of his supervisor, the lawyer. One wall separates Bartleby from his co-workers in the other room. A partition separates Bartleby from his supervisor's desk. Bartleby does have a small window in his cubicle, but it faces the building next door, giving him only a brick wall to look at. Few people visit, other than the occasional client, and there are few disruptions to the daily routine.

The office setting has often been compared to a "dungeon." Readers point out that Bartleby's location, surrounded on all sides by walls, isolates him from humanity. It has been suggested by more than one critic that Bartleby's eventual refusal to work stems from his oppressive surroundings. It is tempting to read the setting as a symbolic presentation of autistic alienation. The setting is surely open to this interpretation.

But for some individuals on the spectrum, this work environment would be ideal. Rather than isolation, this setup provides Bartleby with solitude, which might be a nice contrast to the noisy, crowded, chaotic city that surrounds him. Rather than dreariness, perhaps this environment gives Bartleby a measure of calm by allowing his senses to heal and decompress. Who knows what kind of horrible environment he was in before he found this job? Copying documents all day long would surely be seen as a boring job to most neurotypicals, but to a person with AS, the predictable rhythm and repetition might be appealing. In this island of peace in the middle of New York City, Bartleby has found a secure place to be himself.

Further evidence that this setting "works" for Bartleby is the fact that he spends evenings and weekends at the office, essentially moving in. If this environment were hostile or unkind to Bartleby, he would surely seek other living arrangements when not working. Additionally, when the lawyer lets Bartleby go midway through the story, Bartleby wants to stay right where he is. Donna Williams, an author who has autism, described a job she once had working in the storage room of a department store. Her job was putting items on shelves, organizing shelves, and finding things for people—she enjoyed the quiet respite from the world and the sense of calm order that this situation provided for her—she much preferred it to working in the bustling, unpredictable, people-filled department store outside. This seems to be the case for Bartleby as well. One wonders what would have happened if the lawyer had just let Bartleby stay in the office behind his partition. He certainly wasn't hurting anybody.

Characterization

The three office workers (other than Bartleby) are presented in 2-D, cartoon like fashion. Turkey is an alcoholic who is sober in the morning and drunk in the afternoon. Nippers has chronic indigestion: in the morning he is irritable, but in the afternoon he is calm. Ginger Nut is an errand boy who brings the other workers cookies. Beyond that, there is no development of these three characters. This "flatness" resembles the portrayal of minor characters in Hans Christian Andersen's fairy tales or in Lewis Carroll's *Alice in Wonderland.*

The title character, Bartleby, provides a good example of how writers on the spectrum usually create interesting characters that are also on the spectrum. It is very easy to see how Bartleby fits the profile of a person with Asperger's Syndrome. The lawyer himself recognizes that Bartleby does not deliberately cause problems in the office, but that he is "a little deranged" (33) and his eccentricities are "involuntary" (11). Bartleby shows Aspergen impairment in four areas of his life.

For one thing, his social skills are problematic: he seems to have no ties to family, and he clearly has no friends. He does not mix with his co-workers, and he is unable to accept his supervisor's kindly overtures. The lawyer observes that Bartleby is "alone, absolutely alone in the universe. A bit of wreck in the mid-Atlantic" (20).

Second, his communication skills are also not typical. He does not initiate conversation, nor does he speak unless spoken to. When he does talk, he falls into an echolalic pattern of repeating "I would prefer not to" numerous times in the story. He uses the expression as a catch-all phrase, rather than communicating more directly his needs or wishes. His voice has an odd pitch to it, and is described as "flute-like."

Bartleby is also unable to think outside of a rigid pattern, which is typical of AS individuals. He can't give an explanation for *why* he prefers not to work. He can't say what he would like to do instead. He can't bring himself to go for a walk, visit a nearby park, look for a new job, or ask the lawyer for a different task to do. His world is binary. He can copy, or he can prefer not to copy, but life seems to offer him no other possibilities. At the story's end, but two choices remain to him: either living in the lawyer's office, or dying in the prison. His choices are restricted and he cannot imagine any other options.

We are given less information about Bartleby's sensory impairments. We know that he has vision problems (like people in Melville's family). We know that he is on a very limited diet, apparently subsisting on only cookies and cheese. When he is offered a special meal in the prison, he counters by saying, "It would disagree with me; I am unused to dinners" (32), indicating that he isn't much interested in food at all. He appears not to have any motor clumsiness, and his handwriting is neat and legible.

All in all, Bartleby is portrayed as an autistic hero in this story. The sensory problems, rigid thinking, communication problems, and social impairments all point to his place on the spectrum. Many of the traits he exhibits are those that Melville himself also had. Bartleby's very existence points to the fact that Asperger's Syndrome has been around for some time, even if a name for it had not yet been provided when Melville wrote this story.

The other main character in the story, the lawyer, is a reasonably well developed character for a 19th century short story. The lawyer is the most interesting character in the story, it seems to me. He provides steady work for four people, and expects steady work from them in return. But from the moment that Bartleby first utters "I would prefer not to," the lawyer is faced with a quandary about how he should handle the insubordination. Bartleby's "passive resistance" is extremely frustrating for everyone in the office (some critics speculate that his character might be based on Thoreau, who also practiced passive resistance in response to authority). The lawyer hires Bartleby, but cannot let Bartleby stay on without pulling his weight. He is annoyed by Bartleby, yet obviously feels compassion toward him as well. He tries to be firm, he tries to be gentle. In the end, he abandons Bartleby to his own devices, leaving him to a solitary death in the "Tombs." Every time I teach this story, my students always end up debating the same question: how much responsibility does the lawyer have toward Bartleby? Has he done enough? Should he do more for him? What else can be done? Is Bartleby's death his fault?

Personal Themes

The story gives itself up to many possible readings. Critics have argued that the story of a poor worker who dies of self-imposed starvation is a Marxist critique of capitalism; a Christian story of martyrdom; or a sympathetic account of a frustrated writer. But another way of reading this story, the way I read it, is that Melville has, on the surface, written the story of a man with Asperger's Syndrome who is having problems in the world of work. On a deeper, more personal level, it is also the story of Melville's own inability to foster a satisfying relationship with his father. In other words, the story was written as a way for Melville to come to terms with his own AS condition and to examine how it impacted his life, both at work and at home.

Asperger's Syndrome in the Work Place

Melville experienced many AS-related problems at the work place. For one thing, he did not interview well. One biographer noted that "Given the number of unsuccessful job searches to his credit, one wonders if he failed to make a good impression on the interviewer" (Robertson-Lorant 67). He trained to do surveying, but when he applied for surveying jobs he did not get them, perhaps because the company thought he was "flighty or truculent" (Delbanco 27). He worked as an errand-boy in a bank, but decided that working indoors in an office was "claustrophobic drudgery" (Robertson-Lorant 70). He tried teaching for a while, but could not manage to discipline the students. His work performance was no doubt hindered by the fact that he was a heavy drinker, as many Asperger individuals are (Tinsley and Hendrickx).

Life at sea was a good option for Melville, and he spent several years of his young manhood working on ships, including cargo vessels and whaling ships. Young Herman signed up as a cabin boy on a ship that sailed to Liverpool, and found that life on board ship suited him. Next he signed up to work a whaling ship—midway through that tour of duty he jumped ship and spent weeks living on a Pacific island with a tribe of cannibals, only to escape them by joining another ship that was passing by. The freedom of living outside of society's rules, the easy camaraderie found in a population of men at sea, and a life of physical labor lived outside in the fresh air all agreed with him. The social codes and rules of the city were left far behind and his AS was not a problem for him on these ships.

The other career that worked well for Melville was writing. Like other AS authors in this study, Melville's love for writing became an obsession in his life, and he enjoyed a "characteristic addiction to writing long hours in the attic" (McCarthy 95). While working on projects he would spend up to 12 hours a day working, often in a tiny attic room away from distractions. It is easy to see how this kind of work would appeal to a man like Melville—no boss, no co-workers, no petty rules to keep track of. There is room for creativity, but on one's own terms. There is joy in creating a thing of beauty. There is pride and a sense of accomplishment.

Which brings us back to Bartleby, whose repetitious work tasks inspired neither creativity, nor pride, nor joy.

The lawyer needs to hire someone who can neatly and accurately copy documents for him. He has advertised the position in the paper, and Bartleby shows up at the office for an interview. The lawyer describes Bartleby as being "motionless...pallidly neat, pitiably respectable, and incurably forlorn" (6). Anyone who has been in a hiring position knows that sometimes the job goes to the applicant one feels sorry for rather than the person one is impressed by. Bartleby has had one job previous to this: at the Dead Letter office of the US Post Office, but the lawyer doesn't discover this until later. There is no mention of other work experience or education. The lawyer is merely glad that Bartleby appears to be "sedate" in contrast to the other office employees.

Bartleby does not mingle with the other workers in the office. Both Turkey and Nippers have their own individual quirks, and it seems that they would be receptive to having Bartleby join them at lunch time or after work, but he stays behind his screen and ignores them. When Bartleby refuses to do his job, they eventually grow hostile toward him and even begin to ridicule him for his strangeness. Nippers thinks the lawyer should "kick him out of the office." Ginger Nut says that Bartleby is "a little luny."

Why does he stop working? Perhaps he does not like having his day defined by other people. Perhaps he is just tired and worn out. Perhaps he has some kind of illness and doesn't feel well. Perhaps he is overcome by a depression so severe that he cannot say yes to anything—he can only say no. The problem is, we will never know what really troubles the man because he is not equipped with the communication skills he needs to define his problem, share it with others, and ask for help. This inability to communicate needs is unfortunately common among AS people.

One wonders how closely Melville identified with this strange and provocative character. Biographer Delbanco saw a connection: "Perhaps some precipitating event in Melville's life might explain the half-despondent, half-delirious mood of this remarkable story" (219) and biographer Arvin also considered that "something of Melville's own plight is obviously reflected here" (242). In a sense, Bartleby and Melville were both writers, earning a living with their pens. Like Bartleby, Melville was not cut out for office work even though Gansevoort and Allan, two of his brothers, were lawyers. He did not seem to enjoy any feelings of camaraderie with co-workers when he worked clerical jobs. But what about Melville's response to persons of authority? What might the relationship between Bartleby and the lawyer, his supervisor, reveal to us?

Clearly, the lawyer represents more than just an employer. On a symbolic level, the lawyer also becomes an authority figure in the story. In this all-male office, a space that runs on patriarchal authority, the relationship between Bartleby and his employer becomes a re-enactment of an unhappy relationship between a traditional "neurotypical" father and his quirky "AS" son. The relationship is not satisfying for either: the father feels frustrated, inadequate, and guilty; the son feels helpless, rejected, and unloved. This relationship was inspired, no doubt, by the stormy relationship that Melville had with his own father, Allan Melville. In real life, as in the story, the son felt utterly abandoned by the father who never understood him.

The Father–Son Relationship

Herman was a second son, in a time when primogeniture was still prevailing socially, if not legally. Herman's older brother Gansevoort was clearly the favorite child—good looking, intelligent, dashing—he was the one Allan and the Melville clan placed their hopes and dreams on. Apparently Allan didn't think too much of young Herman, whose AS traits must have perplexed the father: he referred to Herman as a "slow and backward child" (Robertson-Lorant 596) and was "not particularly impressed" with Herman's intellectual abilities (76). Allan was too strict with the boy, wielding the rod often as punishment. He was inconsistent, sometimes beating Herman and sometimes coddling him. Herman felt neglected by his father, and was devastated by the fact that his father never showed him love (Robertson-Lorant 48). Allan's early death when Herman was only 12 felt like the ultimate abandonment, and Herman never came to terms with this. All his life, he felt unloved, angered, and frustrated as a result.

I believe this sadly unsatisfying father–son relationship, made more complicated by Herman's place on the autism spectrum, provides the emotional center of the short story "Bartleby." Herman's feelings of neglect and abandonment are echoed in his portrayal of the forlorn scrivener, whose "miserable friendlessness and solitude are here revealed" (15). Clearly Bartleby, like young Herman, needs some kind of assistance, but he does not know how to go about getting it. He is stuck in the pattern he has cut out for himself, and can't figure out how to change it. He cannot find the language to express what he must be feeling inside. He can't find his way out from behind the wall. He continues to hope that the lawyer will understand him.

What does Bartleby offer his employer? His loyalty. Bartleby has formed a heart-breaking attachment to his employer, and once the attachment is formed, Bartleby sticks to the man like glue. He wants to stay near him. He wants to live in the office. In his own way, he is staying true to the "friendship" even though he can no longer do the required work. I have seen this kind of loyalty before. I have seen my AS son, in middle-school, remain steadfastly devoted to his favorite science teacher throughout the year, spending before-school time, lunch time, and after-school time in her room. Sometimes he did odd jobs for her, sometimes he worked on homework or science projects, but for the most part he was content to just sit in the corner while she worked. He felt safe in her room. He liked being near her. When 7th grade came to an end, he cried.

I think I know how Bartleby felt when the lawyer up and moved away—betrayed, abandoned, worthless. "Since he will not quit me, I must quit him," the lawyer concludes. "I will change my offices; I will move elsewhere; and give him fair notice, that if I find him on my new premises I will then proceed against him as a common trespasser" (27). The ending of "Bartleby" breaks my heart. I wish there had been another way to end the story. Which is surely how young Melville, at age 12, must have felt when his father passed away. Alone, adrift, a "bit of wreck in the mid-Atlantic."

Just as art imitates life, so does life imitate art, at times. The story of Bartleby, a re-telling of Melville's agonizingly distant relationship with his father, becomes also a prediction of the relationship he was to have with his own sons, Malcolm and Stanwix. At the time that Melville wrote "Bartleby" he was the father of two young boys, and the role of father was not easy for him. Like his own father, Melville was sometimes too strict with his boys. Like his own father, he sometimes did not pay enough attention to them, and was "dangerously inconsistent" in his parenting. (Robertson-Lorant 370). It is clear that Melville loved them, but without the role model of a father in his own life, he seemed unsure about how to develop a good relationship with his boys. As Malcolm passed his teen years and became a young man, Melville had no map to guide him in the dance between father and son. In 1867, at age 18, Malcolm committed suicide by shooting himself in the head. Melville understood that the blame for this tragedy was partly his responsibility. In another story, *Billy Budd*, Melville was to write of a young man driven to suicide by his father.

"Melville's fiction illustrates the depth of his understanding of abnormality and the integrity, determination, and art with which he expressed that understanding" (McCarthy 142). Melville's understanding of how his own "abnormality" affected his roles as worker and father provided rich material for the literature he was to write. Long after we have finished reading the story of Bartleby the scrivener, the words "I would prefer not to" continue to echo in our hearts. Characters like Bartleby—both loyal and stubborn—remind us that "those with autism show us how they determine the tenor of their lives, and in so doing ignore and escape the many narratives that would contain and define them, and turn them into something else" (Murray 23). Melville was correct to provide an ending for his story that lets Bartleby remain Bartleby, a character driven like Melville by integrity and determination, no matter how much the lawyer, or others, might wish that he would change.

Works Cited

Arvin, Newton. *Herman Melville.* New York: Grove Press, 1950.

Delbanco, Andrew. *Melville: His World and His Work.* New York: Knopf, 2005.

Fitzgerald, Michael. *The Genesis of Artistic Creativity: Asperger's Syndrome and the Arts.* London: Jessica Kingsley Publishers, 2006.

McCarthy, Paul. *The Twisted Mind: Madness in Herman Melville's Fiction.* Iowa City: University of Iowa Press, 1990.

Melville, Herman. "Bartleby the Scrivener: A Story of Wall Street." http://www.gutenberg.org/etext/11231.

Murray, Stuart. *Representing Autism: Culture, Narrative, Fascination.* Liverpool: Liverpool University Press, 2008.

Robertson-Lorant, Laurie. *Melville: A Biography.* New York: Clarkson Potter Publishers, 1996.

Tinsley, Michael and Hendrickx, Sarah. *Asperger Syndrome and Alcohol.* London: Jessica Kingsley Publishers, 2008.

CHAPTER FIVE

Emily Dickinson

Emily Dickinson

Like Herman Melville, Emily Dickinson (1830–1886) never received recognition for literary brilliance during her lifetime, but in her case it was because she wrote in secret, sharing only a handful of poems with a small circle of trusted friends and family. Her sister Lavinia was astonished to find over a thousand poems, carefully stitched into tiny booklets, upon unlocking a trunk in the attic after Emily's death. Dickinson's lyrical poetry marks an important turning point in American literature, as she moved away from the heavy philosophical poetry that preceded her and led the way toward a more spontaneous, creative style. Her work was unique, passionate, and child-like, just as she was, and her contribution to American literature is undeniable. Emily Dickinson was an original genius who showed many traits of Asperger's Syndrome (AS)—her place on the spectrum influenced her poetry in several important ways.

Dickinson and Asperger's Syndrome

Dickinson showed both the impairments and gifts typical of those with Asperger's Syndrome. Like most people on the spectrum, she was challenged with sensory issues. She suffered from eye problems (exotropia, or mis-aligned eyes) all of her life. She had very sensitive hearing and had to cover her ears when it thundered, but was also a fine pianist who composed her own music. She suffered from dyspraxia (fine motor clumsiness), and her handwriting was so bad she had to clip labels off packages to tape on letters instead of addressing envelopes herself. Her acute sense of smell caused her headaches, yet she also loved flowers that were heavily scented. She seemed to have no taste for food, which brought her dangerously close to anorexia at times. She could not wear confining clothes, and only wore simple white dresses throughout her adult life.

Dickinson's social quirkiness is well documented: she had problems establishing proper boundaries between herself and other people. As a girl, she was too intense in her friendships with other girls her age, crushing them with her insistent, fervent cries for closeness and love. As an adult, she withdrew from the world and would not venture from the house she grew up in. Her social problems were exacerbated by her difficulties with communication. When company would come to visit, she sometimes conversed with them through a closed door. She had trouble talking to people outside of her family, but was an obsessive correspondent who wrote hundreds and hundreds of letters. Emily's brother and sister also showed signs of AS, and together they were known as the eccentrics of Amherst, Massachusetts: "the brother and sisters all, to varying degrees, ended up somewhat queer, lonely, at odds with the environment, and apart from the community, toward which they developed a defensive hauteur" (Cody 447).

Like others on the spectrum, Dickinson had few interests but she pursued them avidly. As a girl she focused her attention on plants—she pressed local specimens into a remarkable herbarium—and she was passionate about her flower garden. She was deeply moved by music and played the piano well. Most of all, she loved reading and writing. Her father possessed an enormous library, and she read voraciously throughout her life. But the special interest that consumed her passion was writing: she wrote over 1700 poems in her lifetime, a staggering output for someone who died in her fifties.

Her AS no doubt contributed to her literary genius. When it came to writing poetry, Dickinson was dedicated and focused. She found the time, the place, and the energy to write poem after poem, gaining confidence and strength every time she picked up her pen. A neurotypical Emily might have become interested in fashion, in boys, or in the latest entertainments, perhaps writing an occasional poem from time to time. But Dickinson's AS enabled her to focus single-mindedly on poetry, and in this way she was able to develop her gift without distraction.

Dickinson's obsession with writing gave her remarkable dedication to honing her craft as a poet. The poems she wrote were affected by her autism primarily in four ways. She displayed an autistic disregard of audience; a quirky use of language that wrestled against conventions; a reliance on metaphor and symbol; and the exploration of themes and ideas related to autism.

Letters, Poetry, and the Problem of Audience

In addition to writing poetry, Dickinson was a fanatical letter writer (like Andersen, Carroll, and other AS writers). Her letters to 100 individuals must have numbered in the thousands. Letters allowed her to connect meaningfully with others while at the same time avoiding social situations that were hard for her. They also represented her emotional tie to the outside world: "Bearing the full burden of her need for understanding, love, and companionship, letters assumed a prominence in her life far beyond their usual role for more ordinary personalities" (Cody 486). A quick glance at her letters reveals an apprehension of audience that seems to be driven by her Asperger's Syndrome.

Her letters were not typical written communications. They did not convey the usual details of everyday life, or gossip from home, or comments about the weather. Each letter was a carefully crafted opportunity to display a bit of her interests, or to explore a bit of the unknown, or even the unknowable. The letters were filled with philosophical observations and linguistic acrobatics just as Lewis Carroll's were. They frequently presented riddles to untangle since she often focused on self-expression rather than communication. Many people with AS write in an idiosyncratic fashion that privileges the author rather than the reader, and Emily was no exception. Her letters "had a problem of organization and coherence. They abound in energy and zest for living, but they show her groping for direction and meaning...she [either] pummeled and browbeat her correspondents, or bathed them in tender emotions" (Sewall *Life* 240). A letter to her sister-in-law Sue dated 1858 showed her odd epistolary style:

> We wouldn't mind the sun, dear, if it didn't set—How much you cost—how much Mat [Susan's sister] costs—I will never sell you for a piece of silver. I'll buy you back with red drops, when you go away. I'll keep you in a casket—I'll bury you in the garden—and keep a bird to watch the spot—perhaps my pillow's safer—Try my bosom last—That's nearest of them all, and I should hear a foot the quickest, should I hear a foot—The thought of the little brown plumes makes my eye awry. The pictures in the air have few visitors. (Hart 75)

In this letter, Dickinson reminds Sue (again) how much she cares for her. She compares Sue to a sun that she wishes would never set, to something more valuable than silver, to something equally as valuable as Dickinson's own blood. Dickinson's need to hold Sue close has her fantasizing that she might keep Sue as a corpse in her garden, or else keep Sue in her own bed. The image of the "little brown plumes" is a puzzling one, perhaps one known only to the two of them. The last line suggests Dickinson's penchant for fantasy. Clearly Emily was thinking of herself and her own anxiety while writing this letter. One can only wonder what Sue's response to this was.

Dickinson's poems, even more than her letters, show a disregard for the reader. Since most of her poems never made it outside of her attic room, it is reasonable to assume that she wrote them mainly for herself and her own pleasure. Rather than tools for communication, they were objects of self-expression and artistic self-fulfillment. They served as a prayer to the universe more than a mode of communication to other people. As Fitzgerald observes: "[Autistic] writing is often tailored more to the writer than to the reader: they don't always help the reader with information so that he or she can follow the topic" (Fitzgerald 28). Many of her poems make obscure references or have gaps in meaning. They leapfrog from one idea to another with a transition that might be clear in Dickinson's mind but does not make it to the page. Consider this small poem (poem 242):

It is easy to work when the soul is at play—
But when the soul is in pain—
The hearing him put his playthings up
Makes work difficult—then—

It is simple, to ache in the Bone, or the Rind—
But Gimblets—among the nerve—
Mangle dantier—terribler—
Like a Panther in the Glove—

The first two lines are straightforward—the speaker works well when happy, not so well when sad. Line three shows an unusual pronoun—"him" seems to refer to the speaker's soul once again, but since the author is female this choice of pronoun is puzzling. Still, we understand that "play" and "work" are closely related for the speaker.

In the second stanza, Dickinson makes a leap that some readers might not be able to follow. When the speaker claims that it is "simple" to ache in the bone or rind (the body, presumably), she seems to be saying that physical pain is something that can be managed, although these lines are open to other interpretations. The next image, "gimblets," refers to a small drilling tool—presumably this is a metaphor for another kind of pain, a sharper one that "mangles" the nerves. This kind of pain has no remedy. But with the final image, Dickinson skips from a Yankee workshop to a wild animal in the jungle. Is the "panther in the glove" a reference to another kind of pain? Why a panther? Is the pain wrapped in cozy wool? Could this be a reference to the pain inflicted by someone she loves, perhaps? What about the work mentioned in the first line? Since this poem ends with a dash rather than a period, the reader is left hanging. There is no title to help us. Some kind of resolution is wanting here.

Modern readers are more accustomed to these kinds of dissonant leaps and gaps in meaning. We are familiar with the fragment in artwork. We can be comfortable with ambiguity. But when we consider that this poem was written in 1861, Dickinson's peculiar poetics is astounding. Compare her poem to these stanzas written by Julia Ward Howe at about the same time:

The World I am Passing Through
Few, in the days of early youth,
Trusted like me in love and truth.
I've learned sad lessons from the years;
But slowly, and with many tears;
For God made me to kindly view
The world that I was passing through.

How little did I once believe
That friendly tones could e'er deceive!
That kindness, and forbearance long,
Might meet ingratitude and wrong!
I could not help but kindly view
The world that I was passing through.

And though I've learned some souls are base,
I would not, therefore, hate the race;
I still would bless my fellow men,
And trust them, though deceived again.
God help me still to kindly view
The world that I am passing through!

Howe is aware of her readers and gives us the clues we need to understand her message. The title, the clear declarative statements, the conventional punctuation, and the repetition of "I could not help but kindly view/the world that I was passing through" all contribute to a successful communication with the reader. This author has been hurt, like Dickinson, but still believes that God will help her keep a positive outlook.

Julia Ward Howe's poem is the more successful of the two if we are measuring the writer's ability to clearly convey a meaning from writer to reader. And yet, viewed side by side, Emily Dickinson's poem has a vitality, a deep passion, and an enigmatic creativity that makes it the better work of art. Emily was far ahead of her time in this respect. She was one of the first to herald in the "art for art's sake" movement that was to follow her at the turn of the 20th century. Today, her poetry—and her letters—are now highly esteemed, not merely as tools of communication, but as works of art.

Dickinson's Battle with Conventional Poetic Form

Editor Thomas Higginson's observation of Dickinson as a young woman reveals much about her unconventional language/communication skills:

> She came toward me with two day-lilies, which she put in a childlike way into my hand, saying softly, under her breath, "These are my introduction," and adding, also under her

> breath, in childlike fashion, "Forgive me if I am frightened; I never see strangers, and hardly know what I say." But soon she began to talk, and thenceforward continued almost constantly; pausing sometimes to beg that I would talk instead, but readily recommencing when I evaded...she seemed to speak absolutely for her own relief, and wholly without watching its effect on her hearer...she went on talking constantly. (Linscott 18)

This "conversation" shows how awkwardly Dickinson communicated with someone she did not know. She communicated through objects, at first, then as she warmed up to her special interest (poetry) she proceeded to lecture one-sidedly, based only on her need to talk. This passage presents a text-book description of an AS person's difficulties with language and communication. Higginson concludes: "the impression undoubtedly made on me was that of an excess of tension, and of something abnormal" (Linscott 20). That "abnormality" was Asperger's Syndrome.

Just as her spoken communication patterns were not typical, so were her written communication patterns also seen as quirky or eccentric. Much has been written about Dickinson's unconventional writing style. Feminist critic Lissa Holloway-Attaway and others suggest that she "uses a disjunctive method of communication, that the poet's revision of the rules of grammar thwart the reader's expectations of normal, ordered language" and goes on to explain that this disjunction is her deliberate attempt to "revise fundamental cultural inequities" ("Business of Circumference" 185). Holloway-Attaway suggests that, by dismantling the language, Dickinson is also dismantling patriarchal power. Although I like this explanation, I really don't think she put much thought into this kind of political action. Rather, I think that her unconventional style was a manifestation of the language/communication differences she experienced as a result of her place on the autistic spectrum. She stubbornly resisted cultural expectations and felt compelled to do things her own way.

This stubbornness about breaking literary conventions is a trait shared by many AS writers: "There is no doubt that in a literary sense there is something distinctive and unusual in their literary works. They produce a kind of autistic/Asperger-type written language and dialogue" (Fitzgerald 28). It could be these AS writers feel that their way of writing is superior to the mainstream way, as would be the case with Thoreau. It could be that they enjoy going against the grain because it is stimulating in some way, as would be the case with Lewis Carroll (not to mention my AS son's benchmark exam written in "hillbilly" dialect). It could also be that they have tapped into an exhilarating energy that comes from creating *avant-garde* art, as would be the case with James Joyce. I believe all three motives were behind Dickinson's unconventional style.

The critics of her era faulted her poetry for not adhering to the rules of poetic form. She used rhyme, but also used near-rhyme (rhyming "home" with "tune") and sight-rhyme (rhyming "butterfly" with "carefully") which some people assumed was an accident, or a lack of control, rather than a deliberate breaking free of the chains of consistency. Consider the Dickinson poem quoted above, which rhymes "pain" with "then" and "nerve" with "glove." This kind of off-rhyme was not being used by very many poets at the time; years later, it was to become very common. Today, Julia Ward Howe's exact sing-song rhymes seem naïve and too predictable to a modern sensibility.

Dickinson understood how to control her rhythm pattern, often using the 4/3/4/3 stressed beats rhythm pattern of ballads or old hymns. The first stanza of her poem cited above follows this rhythm pattern perfectly:

It is easy to work when the soul is at play—(4 stressed beats)
But when the soul is in pain—(3)
The hearing him put his playthings up(4)
Makes work difficult—then—(3)

But what happens in the next stanza? The rhythm becomes garbled, the pattern falls apart. We are unsure of how to read the closing line:

It is simple, to ache in the Bone, or the Rind—(4)
But Gimblets—among the nerve—(3)
Mangle dantier—terribler—(3?)
Like a Panther in the Glove—(?)

Is this rhythmic inconsistency an error? Of course not. She is manipulating the form to follow the sense. The happy line "It is easy to work when the soul is at play" follows a perfect anapest rhythm all the way across. The hurting last line "Like a Panther in the Glove" seems to stumble over a trochaic beat. Just as her nerves are falling apart, so is her rhythm pattern.

The poets who followed Dickinson are indebted to her for showing them how to create one's own form, the form that best suits the subject matter or emotions, rather than slavishly following a set pattern. She shows us all that it's ok to break the rules, ok to stubbornly follow one's own poetic drumbeat. Consider this Dickinson stanza from poem 706, which sounds as modern as a stanza from Sylvia Plath:

I cannot live with you,
It would be life,
And life is over there
Behind the shelf

When she showed her poetry to Higginson, he recommended that she pay closer attention to form. She ignored him. Publisher Houghton Mifflin rejected her poems as "Too queer—rhymes all wrong" and they thought Higginson, who submitted them on her behalf, "must be getting out of his mind to recommend such stuff" (Sewall *Life* 293). She was, like many geniuses, ahead of her time. Dickinson's

AS gave her the necessary eccentricity to be unconventional and also the courage to ignore the opinions of others.

Dickinson's Rich Use of Simile, Metaphor, and Symbol

Donna Williams takes offense at the false assumption that people on the spectrum cannot create or understand metaphors. In fact, she says that because she processes sensory information in a different way than neurotypical people do, she always thinks associatively, experiencing many things in her world as physical representations of other things—symbolic objects, in a sense. As she explains in her website, for her, an elevator with tiled walls is like a bathroom; a lecture room with a heat vent is like a clothes dryer; a necklace with a shiny black stone is like a television screen. When Williams is confronted with something unfamiliar, she understands what it is and how it works by comparing it to something familiar. She explains how thinking metaphorically helps her process incoming information and how it helps her make sense out of the chaotic world she inhabits:

> ...It seems to me my world is like a big string of metaphors, that I live in a big string of metaphors and that the rest of the world sees things based on meaning, literal meaning, but let me tell those of you with the luxury to rely on eyes and ears that can interpret fluently and broadly, the world of someone with receptive processing challenges is one where you make whatever close matches you can and many are nothing like you'd make if you could process fluently for interpretive meaning. So do I understand metaphor? I think so.

Metaphors are crucial for her—she probably would not be able to understand neurotypical "reality" without them. In her autobiographies, Williams creates and uses metaphors as tools for understanding herself, the world, and her place in the world. Like

Williams, Emily Dickinson also relied on metaphor and symbol to help her make sense out of a world that was often too overwhelming to process in other ways.

Nearly every time Dickinson put her pencil to paper, she used figurative devices. Some of these were highly personal symbols that only she could interpret. Others were somewhat easier to figure out for a reader willing to do a little research. Some were universal symbols that other writers also used (flowers, animals, natural objects, religious references). Communicating through metaphor had the advantage of allowing her to evoke an idea without directly stating it. She could toss out an idea "in disguise" and make herself less vulnerable in the process. This method appeals to many people with autism spectrum disorders who are often uncomfortable with directly stating their thoughts or feelings to other people.

Like many of the other authors in this study, especially Andersen and Yeats, Dickinson created metaphors to represent the neurological condition that set her apart from other people. She didn't have the phrase "Asperger's Syndrome" in her "lexicon," but she knew she was different, and quite often she felt isolated and alienated from other people. One of the metaphors she used most often to depict these feelings was the image of the little boat (or swimmer) lost at sea.

The sea often presents a menacing force in her poetry. Consider these images: in one poem she walks her dog "and visited the sea," and as the tide moves in it threatens to drown her: "But no man moved me till the tide/ Went past my simple shoe/ And past my apron and my belt/ And past my bodice too" (poem 656). The forceful, overwhelming ocean slowly rises up toward her chin, but her feet remain in place and she can not run away, swim, or save herself. In another poem, a drowning person struggles but can not survive: "Drowning is not so pitiful/ As the attempt to rise/ three times, tis said, a sinking man/ Comes up to face the skies/ And then declines forever" (poem 1542). The chaos of the vast, mysterious cosmos is too much for her, just as the outside physical world is sometimes "too much" for a person with autism. She cannot help but drown.

In another poem, Dickinson portrays a small boat that has left the shore to struggle bravely against the all-powerful sea: "It tossed and tossed/ A little brig I knew/ O'ertook by blast/ It spun and spun/ And groped delirious, for morn." Although the boat struggles, it is no match for the ocean: "It slipped and slipped/ as one that drunken stepped/ Its white foot tripped/ Then dropped from sight" (poem 746). It's a hopeless image she creates here, an image of helplessness and despair. Many individuals on the spectrum become depressed, and an atypically high number of them commit suicide when they find they cannot cope with the stress of their situations. Was Dickinson suicidal? We have no evidence of this, but we do know that she was obsessed with death. In one poem, the swimmer finds a watery grave: "The stray ships passing spied a face/ Upon the waters borne/ With eyes in death still begging raised/ And hands beseeching thrown" (poem 227). I am reminded here of Lewis Carroll's Alice swimming in a pool of her own tears, or Melville's Captain Ahab drowning in the cold sea, or Hans Christian Andersen's little mermaid dissolving into the ocean's frothy foam. Like these characters, Dickinson struggled against a foe that she could neither understand nor conquer.

Metaphor allowed Emily Dickinson to speak her truth but also to veil it from others: "she had found a way, through the language of figure and metaphor, to protect herself and to work around and ultimately transcend all that was frustrating her emerging view of life, not only her sense of reality and truth but all her minor irritations" (Sewall *Life* 396). No matter what her motives were for using figurative language, her poems are certainly the richer for it.

Dickinson's Autistic Themes

1. A Preference for Solitude

Unable to find peace in the company of society, Emily Dickinson chose solitude, just as Thoreau did. She chose the company of herself, her books, and her poems over the intrusive, confusing society of the world. But in drawing a clear boundary between herself and the world, she was making a conscious choice to do what she needed to do for her own peace of mind, her own emotional survival. R. P. Blackmur once suggested that Dickinson's seclusion was a sort of default second-best lifestyle under the circumstances: "she found herself a shut-in, which was the best she could do with finding herself in the beginning a shut-out" (Sewall *Collection* 82). I would prefer to see her creation of a safe environment as a positive act of self-love, rather than "the best she could do."

Poem 1570 comments on her emotional independence in a positive way:

> How happy is the little Stone
> That rambles in the Road alone,
> And doesn't care about Careers
> And Exigencies never fears—
> Whose Coat of elemental Brown
> A passing Universe put on,
> And independent as the sun,
> Associates or glows alone,
> Fulfilling absolute Decree
> In casual simplicity—

To be "as independent as the sun" is a perfect simile to describe the emotional sustainability that Dickinson is seeking. She imagines that she will truly be happy once she has learned how to live without a need or desire for society.

2. A Special Interest: Reading and Writing

Individuals with AS are known to have a narrow range of cognitive interests, usually called "special interests." One of Dickinson's special interests was books—both reading them and writing them. Like many AS people she was an avid reader who enjoyed novels, non-fiction books, poetry, and the periodicals of her time. Literature could gently and painlessly lead her out to the world, as she says in this poem:

> There is no Frigate like a Book
> To take us Lands away
> Nor any Coursers like a Page
> Of prancing Poetry—
> This Traverse may the poorest take
> Without oppress of Toll—
> How frugal is the Chariot
> That bears the Human Soul—
> (poem 1286)

It's no surprise that she spent a great deal of time reading her own and her father's books, as well as any she could borrow from others. She makes it clear on several occasions that she loves books so much she thinks of them as friends:

> Unto my Books—so good to turn—
> Far ends of tired Days—
> It half endears the Abstinence—
> And Pain—is missed—in Praise...
>
> I thank these Kinsmen of the Shelf—
> Their Countenances Kid
> Enamor—in Prospective
> And satisfy—obtained
> (poem 512)

She enjoys her books in their entire splendor: how they sit on the shelf and wait for her each day, how they turn their "kid" leather faces to greet her, how they bring her satisfaction and even affection. That she saw herself not just as a poet but also as a writer of books is clear from the way she grouped her poems together by theme, stitching them into little booklets, or fascicles; hundreds of them were found after her death.

3. An Obsession with Death

One of the more common traits of Asperger's Syndrome is to become obsessive about an anxious idea or concern. Dickinson's intense interest in death and violence is an example of such a fixation and is well documented. When Emily was 13, her friend Sophia Holland died of a brain fever—Dickinson visited the corpse, and stayed by its side so long she had to be led away. She was known to avidly read death notices in the paper, and seemed to enjoy discussing death in her correspondences with people who had lost a loved one. A friend of hers, Joseph Lyman, wrote to his fiancée that Dickinson could be "rather morbid and unnatural" (Sewall *Life* 426).

One critic noticed the prominence of death imagery in poems of Dickinson, "whose necrophilic preoccupation outdoes everybody except perhaps Poe" (Cody 35). At least 28 poems were about death, while many others referred to it. Sometimes she wrote about her own death, imagining herself either to be dying or dead ("I heard a fly buzz when I died"). Sometimes she wrote about death in the general sense ("Death is like the insect"). She also wrote about the deaths of people she knew ("When I was small a woman died"). Related themes that fascinated her included immortality, afterlife, and heaven. Michael Fitzgerald makes the observation that "persons with Asperger's syndrome and genius are very often concerned about immortality, or about dying before they have achieved their potential. This gives their creative work a sense of urgency" (14). Her poetry was thus both an agent for exploring ideas of death and also, by giving her immortality, of resisting it.

The Brain Poems: Two Kinds of Brains

Emily Dickinson's poetry reveals her awareness that her beautiful, creative mind was not like the more typical minds of others. Her poetry explores two kinds of brains: the neurotypical brain and the brain that is influenced by autism. Consider poem 563:

> The Brain, within its Groove
> Runs evenly—and true—
> But let a Splinter swerve—
> 'Twere easier for You—
>
> To Put a Current back—
> When Floods have slit the Hills—
> And scooped a Turnpike for Themselves—
> And trodden out the Mills—

The neurotypical brain stays "within its Groove" where it "Runs evenly—and true" (poem 563). Dickinson's mind, in contrast, *swerves:* in typical AS fashion, her mind leaves the expected path and boldly goes its own way, bobbing along in its own currents, flooding a hillside with silt, destroying mills, and scooping out a turnpike just for itself. Her brain was unique, and she knew it.

Poem 867 also talks about the brain:

> I felt a Cleaving in my Mind—
> As if my Brain had split—
> I tried to match it—Seam by Seam—
> But could not make them fit—
>
> The thought behind, I strove to join
> Unto the thought before—
> But Sequence raveled out of Sound—
> Like Balls—opon a Floor—

Dickinson says she "felt a Cleaving in [her] Mind." Whereas a neurotypical brain might presumably be "whole," the autistic mind is instead "split." Psychiatrist Lorna Wing characterizes this fragmentation as an autistic lack of "central coherence." Many psychologists have documented the fragmented thought patterns of some AS individuals. Lorna Wing's research has identified certain traits common to autistic minds that may relate to what Dickinson refers to as the "cleaving" of her mind:

> an inability to put together all kinds of information derived from past memory and present events, to make sense of experiences, to predict what is likely to happen in the future and to make plans. People with autistic disorders do not make sense of the world and find it hard to learn from experience. They find it difficult to organize themselves in time and in space. (Wing 4, 5)

Dickinson tries to repair this fragmentation of her brain—tries to line up the pieces and stitch them together "seam by seam" but finds that she cannot "make them fit." When she tries to make sense out of noise (sound) and language (sequence), she can't manage to pull it all together, and the meaning gets away from her like balls of yarn rolling away on a floor. The effort of "mending" her mind causes her a great deal of anguish.

And broken minds cannot always be mended. This seems to be the message of poem 340, in which Dickinson tells us "I felt a Funeral in my Brain."

> I felt a Funeral, in my Brain,
> And Mourners to and fro
> Kept treading—treading—till it seemed
> That Sense was breaking through—
>
> And when they all were seated,
> A Service, like a Drum—
> Kept beating—beating—till I thought
> My mind was going numb—

And then I heard them lift a Box
And creak across my Soul
With those same Boots of Lead, again,
Then Space—began to toll,

As all the Heavens were a Bell,
And Being, but an Ear,
And I, and Silence, some strange Race
Wrecked, solitary, here—

And then a Plank in Reason, broke,
And I dropped down, and down—
And hit a World at every plunge,
And Finished knowing—then—

The image of the funeral indicates that the speaker, Dickinson, has experienced a great loss, coupled with numbness, grief, and despair. This loss causes dark, repetitive thoughts that become obsessive, threatening to destroy her brain. She can't stop her mind from racing.

Several tropes in this poem represent these repetitive thoughts, all of them associated with sound: a drum keeps "beating—beating" until her mind goes "numb." Feet wearing boots of lead trudge back and forth in her mind: they disturb her and "creak across [her] Soul." A bell tolls for the dead, making her feel "wrecked" and "solitary." In each case it is the repetition that she cannot evade, and her obsession leads to destruction.

The destruction is, of course, the breaking of the "plank of reason." Reason was the platform she had cautiously stood upon, but it breaks from the barrage of sound waves caused by drums, footsteps, and bells. It's simply too much—she can't manage the noise. As a woman with AS, Dickinson was prone to sensory sensitivities, especially to noise. The poem's reference to a mental breakdown, or collapse, may have been related to a specific event in her life, such as the death of a loved one or an unfulfilled longing, but the poem also suggests that perhaps her brain isn't as stable or reliable as she would wish.

In poems 445 and 620 Dickinson shows us the world's reaction to someone who is different: *normalize her.* In 445, she remembers that when she was a child, her family "shut me up in Prose" and "put me in the Closet" because they wanted her "still." But Dickinson resists: even though her body may be in "captivity," her brain is still free to "go round." A similar notion of confinement is developed in poem 620, in which the different person is thought to be "straightway dangerous" and is "handled with a Chain." She knows that the "Majority" are the ones who prevail. They set the standard; they confine or punish those who are different. They insist on *normalizing* those who are not normal.

And yet—even though all of these poems mentioned above indicate Emily's knowledge that her mind is unusual, her attitude toward herself seems to be one of stubborn pride, resistance, and self-love, just like Andersen and Thoreau. She knows she is not like others, and she stubbornly takes pride in her difference. When Dickinson says "Much Madness is *divinest* Sense" (my emphasis), she is celebrating her unique mind, her autism, by seeing it as something divine, or holy. She celebrates herself, as we have seen other autistic writers do. Though family or society may confine her to a closet (poem 445), she compares herself to a bird in a cage who can, presumably, fly away at will. In poem 598 she offers the magnificent observation that her brain is "wider than the sky," and "deeper than the sea," and "just the weight of God." She remains confident that her mind can distill "amazing sense from Ordinary Meanings" (poem 446).

Conclusion

In John Cody's psychological assessment of Emily Dickinson, he examined letters, poems, and biographies to support his theory that Emily's big trauma—a mother who did not love her enough—caused Dickinson to have a nervous breakdown, to withdraw from the world, and to write unusual poems. But Cody couldn't figure out what to do with the assessment of her peers—fellow poets—who again and again insisted that Dickinson was simply "born different" with heightened awareness, acute sensory perception, profound intelligence, and a fragile emotional base. In other words, no *outside* trauma caused the differences: she was simply born the way she was—and her behavior was completely normal *for her.* Cody considers their assessment, but argues that the only way these poets could be correct is if Emily had some kind of "new syndrome." Cody's comment, written in 1971, seems to have been reaching forward to the concept of Asperger's Syndrome, which joined the Diagnostic and Statistical Manual of Mental Disorders (DSM-IV) in 1994. A diagnosis of AS perfectly accommodates the observations of Dickinson's peers.

It is very important to recognize Dickinson's place on the autistic spectrum, to appreciate her differences as a person, and to celebrate her special talents as a poet. Emily reminds us of autism's many gifts. Her single-minded focus on writing enabled her to create an enormous *oeuvre* of over 1700 poems; her unconventional thinking patterns inspired her to invent an original writing style that created new rules for punctuation, rhythm, and rhyme; her self-oriented perspective encouraged her to explore the inner workings of the human mind and the secret workings of her own psyche, subject matter that seems thoroughly modern to us now, but was bold and daring back in the 1800s. She is an important part of autistic history and culture, and her poetry has much to teach us about the "complex corridors of the mind" as well as "the secret chambers of the human heart."

Works Cited

Cody, John. *After Great Pain: The Inner Life of Emily Dickinson.* Cambridge: Harvard University Press, 1971.

Fitzgerald, Michael. *The Genesis of Artistic Creativity: Asperger's Syndrome and the Arts.* London: Jessica Kingsley Publishers, 2005.

Franklin, R. W., ed. *The Poems of Emily Dickinson.* Cambridge: Harvard University Press, 1999.

Hart, Ellen Louise and Smith, Martha Nell. *Open Me Carefully: Emily Dickinson's Intimate Letters to Susan Huntington Dickinson.* Ashfield: Paris Press, 1998.

Holloway-Attaway, Lissa. "The Business of Circumference: Circularity and Dangerous Female Power in the Work of Emily Dickinson." *The Emily Dickinson Journal.* Vol. 5, No. 2, Fall 1996. 183–189.

Howe, Julia Ward. "The World I am Passing Through." Found in Rattiner, Susan, ed. *Great Poems by American Women.* New York: Dover, 1998.

Linscott, Robert, ed. *Selected Poems and Letters of Emily Dickinson.* New York: Doubleday Anchor Books, 1959.

Sewall, Richard B, ed. *Emily Dickinson: A Collection of Critical Essays.* Englewood Cliffs: Prentice-Hall, 1963.

Sewall, Richard B. *The Life of Emily Dickinson.* Cambridge: Harvard University Press, 1980.

Williams, Donna. Personal website. www.donnawilliams.net.

Wing, Lorna, MD. *The Autistic Spectrum.* Berkeley: Ulysses Press, 2001.

CHAPTER SIX

Lewis Carroll

Charles Dodgson, Lewis Carroll, and Asperger's Syndrome

Charles Lutwidge Dodgson (1832–1898) was born and raised in rural England, part of a minister's very large family. As Charles Dodgson, he was to grow up to become a great mathematician at Oxford University. Under the pseudonym of Lewis Carroll, he was to become the author of one of literature's most beloved children's books. Carroll was an eccentric, quirky fellow who exhibited several traits of Asperger's Syndrome (AS) as a young boy: he had speech problems (stuttering), perseverative thinking (obsessed with trains, train schedules, time, and riddles), and was something of a loner who preferred daydreaming to playing with other children. Fortunately, he was blessed with a loving family who nurtured his many talents. He was highly intelligent and gifted in the areas of language and mathematics. He loved animals, and considered snails and toads to be his "intimate friends" (Fitzgerald *Genesis* 57). Like many other AS authors, he was a voracious reader who consumed book after book at a young age.

More AS traits emerged when he enrolled at Rugby, a boarding school located far from home. He was clumsy and awkward at team sports, did not mix well with other boys socially, and became rigidly focused on special areas of interest such as word games and math. He was horrified by the ill-mannered habits of the other boys and was often a target of bullying. It was by all accounts the worst period of his life.

As an adult he studied mathematics at Oxford University. Afterwards he was hired as a lecturer and he lived and worked on campus. His awkward social skills, especially his lack of smooth conversational skills, led to his being the "odd man out" most of the time. But the predictable daily routine of university life, coupled with the focus on intellectual and creative pursuits, gave him a lifestyle that suited him well—he was to remain at Oxford for the rest of his life. What had earlier been an interest in reading literature flowered as a career in writing with the success of his first book, *Alice's Adventures in Wonderland.* In many ways he embodied the popular image of the writer as a brilliant but slightly mad man who scribbled in isolation. According to psychiatrist Michael Fitzgerald, there is ample evidence that Carroll had Asperger's Syndrome (see Fitzgerald's *Autism and Creativity* and *The Genesis of Artistic Creativity*).

Carroll's Autistic Writing Process

Analysis of Lewis Carroll's writing process reveals much about the influence of autism on imaginative writing. Most significantly, when he wrote the *Alice* books he employed a writing process that relied greatly on incorporating texts from other authors—in one sense the novel may be read as a "scrapbook" of his favorite works of literature.

Carroll openly tapped into other works through allusion, quotation, satire, and parody. This approach started when he was a boy at home—Carroll edited several family magazines, one of them a 128-page scrapbook called *The Rectory Magazine,* described by Carroll as "A Compendium of the best tales, poems, essays, pictures, etc., that the united talents of the Rectory inhabitants can produce, Edited and printed by C.L.D., fifth Edition, carefully revised, & improved, 1850" (Cohen *Biography* 22). This magazine was a literal scrapbook of family writings, most of them written by Carroll. His writings included jokes, riddles, poetry, and tales—and he alluded to many other writers in his magazine, including Coleridge, Cowper, Crabbe, Dickens, Goldsmith, Gray, Ossian, Scott, Shakespeare, Tennyson, Thomas, and Wordsworth (Cohen, *Biography* 24). Compiling several sources into one book was a process he enjoyed very much.

The *Alice* books have something of a "scrapbook" quality to them as well. Every worthwhile edition of the *Alice* books is accompanied by an extensive set of notes to help the reader identify the outside sources of Carroll's references; without these much of the humor is lost. In the first three short chapters of *Alice's Adventures in Wonderland* alone, there are, according to the Oxford University Press edition, several allusions and references: a reference to a Norman MacLeod poem, a parody of an Isaac Watts poem, a reference to a Latin grammar book, a reference to Haviland Chepmell's English history book, a reference to the *Aeneid*, and a parody of a Robert Southey poem. Parody was his forté.

Thus, the original poem by Isaac Watts,

> How doth the little busy Bee
> Improve each shining Hour,
> And gather Honey all the Day
> From ev'ry op'ning Flow'r

becomes, in Carroll's text,

> How doth the little crocodile
> Improve his shining tail,
> And pour the waters of the Nile
> On every golden scale!

And the song by Robert Southey,

> You are old, Father William, the young man cried,
> The few locks that are left you are grey,

> You are hale, Father William, a hearty old man,
> Now tell me the reason, I pray.

becomes, in Carroll's text,

> You are old, Father William, the young man said,
> And your hair has become very white;
> And yet you incessantly stand on your head—
> Do you think, at your age, it is right?

Many pages of the *Alice* books give more space to the parodies than to Carroll's own writing. Since it is unlikely he made these up while rowing down the river with Alice, he must have consciously added them when he was composing the written version later on.

This "collage" or "mosaic" process is an important aspect of Carroll's writing, as it is for many writers on the spectrum. Since Carroll read widely and had enormous memory capacities, it's almost as though the stored-up memories of texts he had read "spilled out" onto the page. He could not have written in any other fashion. James Joyce is another example of a writer with AS who used a collage technique for writing literature, though to an even greater degree—this is of course famously done in *Ulysses,* but also in *Finnegans Wake*, in which nearly every sentence of the text makes reference to another text. It isn't surprising that Joyce was familiar with the *Alice* books.

This "mimicking" of other texts resembles the "echolalia" that 75% of autistic children who are verbal demonstrate when they are young (Heffner 1). Some children who have autism parrot back everything that is said to them. Some memorize entire passages from television or movies, and are able to "repeat back" everything they've heard with perfect recall later on. There are different reasons why children become echolalic and repeat things orally: some find it either soothing or stimulating, some repeat phrases as a tool for learning language, some use repeated phrases to communicate, some do it to direct their own behavior, some do it just for fun, and others do it for unknown reasons (Heffner 1).

No one has yet studied why writers who are on the spectrum use stored-up words and phrases. In Carroll's case, I believe he simply enjoyed the mental exercise and game-like process of cutting up one text to paste into another. He was a brilliant thinker of the highest order whose mind was in "high gear" all of the time—he was constantly creating puzzles, riddles, brain-teasers, and games for his own—and other people's—amusement. This use of other texts may have become for him a game of "guess the reference," a form of mental challenge.

At one point, incidentally, he *literally* cut and pasted one of his texts. Henry Furniss, who illustrated *Sylvie and Bruno*, recalled a baffling ritual that Carroll created to ensure that nobody but Furniss saw the unpublished manuscript of the poem until it was ready for publication:

> He was determined no one should read his MS but he and I; so in the dead of night (he sometimes wrote up to 4 a.m.) he cut his MS into horizontal strips of four or five lines, then placed the whole of it in a sack and shook it up; taking out piece by piece, he pasted strips down as they happened to come... These incongruous strips were elaborately and mysteriously marked with numbers and letters and various hieroglyphics, to decipher which really would have turned my assumed eccentricity into positive madness! (Cohen *Interviews* 225)

Carroll insisted on following this system until Furniss exploded with frustration and threatened to quit. Only a person with Asperger's Syndrome would treat a professional colleague this way.

Carroll's autism definitely shaped his writing process—but an examination of his literary productions also reveals much about how autism shaped his works of literature. In particular, we find the influence of autism in the areas of narrative strategy, setting, characterization, and use of language.

A Disjointed, Random Narrative Structure

Individuals with AS can be impaired in the area of "central coherence," the ability to formalize a grand over-arching narrative that provides a meaningful framework to otherwise random events. An autistic author's narrative can be seen as a symbolic manifestation of how "autistic persons experience life as an incoherent series of unconnected events" (Rimland xi). We see evidence of this in the way Lewis Carroll structures both *Alice in Wonderland* and *Through the Looking Glass*. The narrative strategy he employs in these works does not provide a plot in the traditional sense. Alice's journey has no overall objective, no special quest. She travels without going anywhere. You could mix up the chapters in almost any order, and the books would be the same. The events also do not build to a crescendo in the way of traditional novels—instead, she wanders from place to place, from adventure to adventure. One event follows the next without a cause and effect relationship. She is not driven by any abstract concept such as loyalty or love or achievement: rather, she "lives in a world of physical particulars" (Blastland 42). Author Michael Blastland, contemplating his own autistic child, muses that "without the conceptual we become lost amid innumerable, unconnected particulars with no relevance beyond themselves" (45). Such a mode of existence can be frightening.

Alice is having a calm and pleasant day with her sister and she is relaxed, even bored. Then she enters Wonderland and there is a sense of panic as she must face numerous rapid shifts in time and place. She has no warning that she is about to fall into a rabbit hole. With the Rabbit's opening words, "Oh dear! Oh dear! I shall be too late!" a pattern of hurrying and rushing is established, and she is swept along so suddenly that she has "not a moment to think about stopping herself." At the bottom of the hole, Alice "suddenly" sees a little three-legged table. Visiting the Duchess later on, a footman in livery "suddenly" comes out of the woods. She stumbles upon the caterpillar by accident. The Duchess speaks to her with a "sudden violence" that makes Alice jump, then later on stops talking, "to

Alice's great surprise." Walking through the woods, she is "startled by seeing the Cheshire-Cat sitting on a bough of a tree."

Carroll's transitions from chapter to chapter are abrupt and unexpected. Alice is rushed from one scene to the next without any opportunity to stop and process what she has just experienced, or to prepare herself mentally for what's to come. This kind of abrupt time change, without transition, is similar to how a day at school feels to a child with AS. There is no flashback, no foreshadowing: since there is only the immediate moment, shifts in time and place are disconcerting and stressful. Carroll captures this feeling of urgency and panic very well.

Feelings of randomness and incompleteness prevail. The story has several loose threads that it never weaves back into the text. In the opening scene, Alice sees a white rabbit who is running around with his watch, late for something. But she never finds out where he's been or where he's going, and she never learns what he'll be late for. She befriends a mouse who starts to share a tale, but he never tells her the ending. A puppy appears out of nowhere, plays fetch with Alice, then runs off and never re-appears. Alice holds a baby that turns into a pig, but who did that baby belong to, anyway? The Duchess? The reader realizes very quickly how absurd it is even to ask questions such as this, for the normal rules do not apply.

Another type of disorientation occurs when time itself moves backwards in Looking-Glass Land (in the sequel to *Alice in Wonderland*). In this story, the White Queen explains to Alice how it works: first we have the punishment, then the crime. First we have the scream, then the injury. We have jam every other day—always yesterday or tomorrow, but never today. Alice says, "It's dreadfully confusing!" To which the Queen replies, "That's the effect of living backwards. It always makes one a little giddy at first." I am reminded here of my student Luke, a man with autism who explained to me why his watch was so important and why he'd be lost without it: "Time is the universe's way of making sure everything doesn't happen at once."

Carroll, like many others with AS, was always fascinated by the concept of time and was constantly trying to figure it out. As a school boy, he sent his sister Elizabeth a letter reminding her to ponder his favorite topic: "Will you answer my questions about clocks when you next write?" (Cohen *Letters* 11). Sometimes, just for fun, he wrote his letters to people with the words arranged in backwards order, from finish to start.

People at Oxford said he bored them by constantly dwelling on the nature of time in conversation: his perseveration on time was no doubt due to his Asperger's Syndrome. His most famous conundrum was this: which would you rather have, a clock that is correct twice each day or once each year? If you answered twice each day, then you've just chosen the broken clock over the one that's only a minute slow.

Time and Space disorientation is an almost constant state of being for many people with autism spectrum disorders. This is one reason why they are often disorganized—because they cannot easily measure or manage time and space. Along these same lines, Carroll himself became fixated on these dimensions and relied heavily on schedules, calendars, lists, schemes, programs, systems, and catalogues. His hyper-organized approach to life left no chance of forgetting or losing anything. One wonders if the disorientation present in the *Alice* books might reflect an underlying nervousness or fear of being overwhelmed by chaos.

Carroll created a story that in some ways defies meaning itself, with its lack of a cohesive narrative. You could shuffle the chapters of his book like a deck of cards and the overall story would not change much. Alice wanders from place to place, unaffected by the people she meets, and unable to affect them. There is no plot, just a series of random events. There is no climax, just an ending. The lack of cohesive narrative on Carroll's storytelling style unmistakably shows the influence of Asperger's Syndrome on his writing.

Setting: Peculiar Harmony, Balance, Orientation

The physical setting of this book, like the time sequence, is neither consistent nor predictable. Alice finds herself in the woods, on a riverbank, in a house, at a table, beside a croquet field, in a courtroom—all seemingly without intermediate transportation or traveling. You could almost argue that Alice stays still while the setting whirls around *her*. The spaces are generic markers to delineate one scene from the next, but there is no personal meaning created in them to transform the spaces into *places*. Alice gets lost several times. Her lack of spatial awareness as she visits Wonderland reminds me of the way AS author Liane Holliday Willey experienced her visit to the university:

> The confusing, rambling, crowded and expansive campus assaulted my limited sense of direction, making it extremely difficult for me to find my way—literally and figuratively—around campus. I remember leaving a class totally unable to discern which way I needed to go in order to follow the most direct path to my next class. The crowds of students would fill the doorways and the halls, giving me little time to grab hold of my thoughts so that usually I would just follow the wave of students out of the buildings, as if I knew where I was going. (48)

Alice, like Lianne, panics when she loses her way.

Like the surrealist artists who followed him, Carroll creates a nonsense world by squeezing and twisting basic design principles such as proportion, balance, harmony, and orientation to create an uneasy, queasy feeling that readers can delight in. Instead of proportion we have disproportion. Alice's body is too big, or else it is too small. Her body becomes so elongated her head must say goodbye to her feet, then suddenly her chin is resting on the ground. Relatively speaking, every time Alice grows or shrinks, the rest of the world changes size accordingly. When she is tiny she meets a caterpillar who appears to be just her size. At one point she shrinks so much that a small puppy appears to be enormous and even life-threatening. Her body grows huge, and the house she is in becomes tiny. The reader is surprised and delighted by this manipulation of proportion, just as adults who return to visit their old kindergarten classroom will laugh when they see how tiny the chairs have become.

Instead of harmony and balance, we find that the landscape is dominated by dissonance and odd juxtapositions. A duchess sits in a room that is perfumed with too much pepper. Alice holds a baby that turns into a lumpy starfish, then a grunting pig. Lobsters dance the quadrille. These associations may have a logical link somewhere, possibly, but that link isn't apparent to Alice or to the reader. Rather, odd combinations appear as they do in the logic of dreams. To the outside observer, these kinds of combinations go together like fish and bicycles. But sometimes there is a method, however strange, to the madness. Michael Fitzgerald believes that the ability to make these unconventional associations is a pre-requisite of intellectual brilliance: "All of these [autistic geniuses he studied] were willing to take intellectual risks by combining what may have looked like unrelated ideas to produce something radically new" (Fitzgerald *Brilliance* 12). It's not surprising, therefore, that Lewis Carroll's avant-garde novel opened up a whole new way of writing books for children—he sprinted from the Victorian era straight through to postmodernism in one amazing text.

The queer setting and physical orientation of these books only adds to the nonsense. In Wonderland, the orientation is flipped over: as Alice falls down through the hole, she realizes that at some point she must be coming out of the earth on the other side. "How funny it'll seem to come out among the people that walk with their heads downward!" she muses. With this in mind, we realize the entire story takes place upside down. I wonder if Carroll was drawing here upon a remembered incident from Rugby: one of the hazing practices was to turn a boy's room "wrong way up" by nailing or gluing everything the boy owned, upside down, to the ceiling (Cohen, *Biography* 19).

In Looking-glass Land, the orientation is reversed: since Alice steps through a mirror, she has entered a world where everything is opposite or backwards. When she finds a copy of Jabberwocky to read, she realizes the printing is a mirror image of how it is supposed to look. Alice realizes that everything is going to be different in this reversed orientation. It is interesting to note here that Carroll's interest in mirror images may have sprung from his own physiognomy: his face was asymmetrical: his eyes and mouth did not "match up" from left to right. He was long preoccupied with reflections, and sometimes wrote letters in mirror-writing to his child friends.

Left/right reversal is a trait that sometimes accompanies autism. An AS boy I know had a very hard time learning right from left, and even as a young man had a hard time with activities that required left/right coordination, such as tying a shoe, skipping, or riding a bike. I recently came upon a passage in Donna Williams' autistic memoir *Nobody Nowhere* that immediately struck me with its similarity to Alice's Looking-glass Land:

> One day I left a building through the same door I had come in, yet I found that somehow the building had changed places. It was not on the same side of the street as before. I walked back into the building, turning my back on the street outside, then I walked back out again. It was still opposite from the way it had been when I had originally gone in... The whole world seemed to have turned itself upside-down, inside out, and back to front. Everything was like a mirror image of what it had been when I had entered the building... Just like driving into a mirror image, I found myself, street after street, at the wrong end, opposite the direction I wanted to go. (Williams 157)

Donna's mirror-disorientation, which occurred during a particularly stressful time in her life, lasted two days, and was very frightening for her.

While some individuals on the spectrum have an excellent memory for places and can read maps very well, others become disoriented when they are in a new place for the first time. The feelings of frustration and anxiety they experience with a change of environment can be overwhelming. Lianne Holliday Willey's disorientation grew progressively worse the longer she stayed in college: "My perception grew more clouded every day. A fog set and would not lift. Spatial difficulties, sensory dysfunction, poor problem-solving skills, over-reliance on my visual thought patterns—the AS kept finding me—even though I never realized it" (50). Alice seems to experience Wonderland in the very same way.

Characterization

Alice's role in novel is to meet and greet the other characters. Although she does have several Asperger traits, she is the "normal" one who acts as the foil to all of the "not so normal" characters around her. She is like the lawyer in Melville's "Bartleby" who befriends the odd man. She is like George Willard in Sherwood Anderson's *Winesburg, Ohio,* who tries to connect with the "grotesques."

The minor characters in Carroll's books are not developed in any meaningful way, and appear only as features of the landscape. Some of them are brilliant figures who lecture and entertain Alice. Some of them are abrupt, rude, or violent. Some are witty and absolutely charming. Some cannot manage a conversation.

She struggles to understand the other characters, whose actions seem arbitrary and unpredictable to her. She complains many times that she is lonely or "all alone." Although she attends a tea party, a croquet game, and a trial, she is unable to figure out the social codes that would help her to fit in. She is unable to participate in conversations with the other characters, as though she does not quite speak their language, or else speaks it in translation. Holliday Willey experienced the same kind of miscommunication. In her autobiography she wrote:

> I think the real problem lay just below the surface of another of my most mysterious and difficult AS traits—my inability to understand my peers' conversations. I understood their language, knew if they had made grammatical errors in their speech, and I was able to make replies to anything that was spoken to me; but, I never came to hear what they were really saying. I never understood their vernacular. (56)

Alice can't quite make out what the Duchess, the Mad Hatter, or Humpty Dumpty are trying to tell her. Throughout the stories, Alice and the other characters struggle with the rules that govern social success: the rules of conversations, of manners, and of games. "It's dreadfully confusing," Alice remarks more than once.

The Duchess

The Duchess is the rudest character in Wonderland, and she demonstrates what Michael Fitzgerald identifies as "autistic aggression," a compulsion toward manipulating and dominating others aggressively, even violently. When Alice visits the Duchess in her house, the Duchess is holding a baby, sneezing, and screaming. When the Duchess first addresses Alice, she calls her a *pig,* "with such sudden violence that Alice quite jumped." Alice makes a comment about cats, to which the Duchess responds again rudely: "You don't know much, and that's a fact!" When Alice talks about the earth's axis, the Duchess yells, "Talking of axes, chop off her head!" She finishes by yelling to Alice, "Oh, don't bother *me*!" all the while tossing the baby "violently up and down." The Duchess often stands way too close to Alice, which bothers her, and the Duchess even rests her chin on Alice's shoulder—people with autism spectrum disorder often have trouble judging personal space boundaries. The Duchess is not capable of showing good manners to her guest. She is tactless, blunt, insensitive, and self-centered.

The Caterpillar

Alice meets a caterpillar who exhibits the pedantic "little professor" conversation skills that typify some people with AS. He sits and smokes a hookah, reminiscent of a pipe-smoking university man. He questions her, contradicts her, and scolds her. He speaks to her "angrily," "contemptuously," and "sternly." He commands her to recite a poem that she presumably memorized in grammar school, then immediately criticizes her performance: "That is not said right," he reprimands. "It is wrong from beginning to end." The constantly commenting caterpillar won't let Alice keep up her end of the conversation: "She had never been so much contradicted in all her life before, and she felt that she was losing her temper."

The caterpillar also resembles Carroll in this way: Lewis Carroll had noticeable problems carrying on conversations, especially with other adults. He was known for steering conversations toward areas that interested him, such as logic, mathematics, or puzzles. If someone brought up a topic he did not care to talk about, he could be quite rude, or even walk away. One man who knew him at Oxford made this observation:

> Dodgson [Lewis Carroll] was not a brilliant talker; he was too peculiar and paradoxical; and the topics on which he loved to dwell were such as would bore many persons; while, on the other hand, when he himself was not interested, he occasionally stopped the flow of a serious discussion by the intrusion of a disconcerting epigram… He could not be relied on to bear his part in the give-and-take of serious conversation—to keep the shuttlecock flying… (Cohen *Interviews* 47)

But with children, who shared his special interests, he was very comfortable and his conversations sparkled.

Humpty Dumpty

Humpty Dumpty is another "little professor" conversationalist. He apparently doesn't make eye contact, because after he exchanges a few lines with her, "Alice didn't know what to say to this: it wasn't at all like conversation, she thought, as he never said anything to *her;* in fact, his last remark was evidently addressed to a *tree.*" When she asks him questions, he treats them like riddles and answers with witty remarks. As he warms to her, however, he makes more of an effort to keep the conversation going, though his self-conscious attempt at socializing is stilted and somewhat amusing: "In that case we start afresh," he says, "and it's my turn to choose a subject." Alice realizes that for him, conversation is a game, not a chance for meaningful interaction. He can't stop spouting the riddles and epigrams. Nonetheless, he's a brilliant, lovable character, who gives us one of literature's greatest lines (although delivered in a *rather* scornful tone): "When *I* use a word, it means just what I choose it to mean—neither more nor less."

The Cheshire Cat

Reserved, stand-offish, smiling, the Cheshire Cat remains a very enigmatic figure. He says very little, only answering questions and speaking when spoken to. His statements are short, declarative, and blunt. When Alice asks, "Would you tell me, please, which way I ought to go from here?" he answers with the all-too-obvious "That depends a good deal on where you want to get to." When she tells him "I don't much care where," then he again replies with an obvious answer: "Then it doesn't much matter which way you go." He seems to be a literal thinker who would rather observe than converse. He remains aloof up in his tree, fading in and out of the story. Alice seems to like him very much (and we are reminded elsewhere that she has a pet cat and is fond of kittens), in spite of his odd communication style.

Language and Games

While children with AS do not like sports, they *do* like games. And Lewis Carroll's brilliant mind was the vehicle for expanding the genre of children's literature to something magical, fun, and original. Before the *Alice* books, children's literature had been didactic, moralistic, and educational. Children weren't supposed to *enjoy* reading; they were supposed to *learn* from it. Carroll shattered this model, and his AS was the hammer that made this possible. He could not have written *Alice* the way he did if he hadn't had Asperger's Syndrome and if he hadn't been his own oddball, wonderful self. As Fitzgerald observed:

> Although human psychologists, in the age of standardization and homogenization, may react suspiciously or adversely to overly peculiar ideas and idiosyncratic people, they should also recognize the rebellious fun in those who march to a different drummer. (Fitzgerald *Autism* 8)

Lewis Carroll didn't just march to a different drummer: he danced the tango.

Carroll loved verbal games and language puzzles that presented a mental challenge. He loved acrostics, riddles, jokes, and verbal brain-teasers. He loved to create, recognize, and ponder paradoxes. He also liked symbolic logic problems. He liked to write things in secret code, in mirror reversal, and in a spiral formation. He also loved toys, gadgets, and inventions, whether he purchased them or created them himself. He was a classic gadgeteer. He was an inventor. And all of this energy infused the *Alice* books with a smart sense of fun—and nonsense.

Carroll especially liked to pose questions that had a "trick" ending that only he, of course, could supply: "The truth about Lewis Carroll is that he was always engaged in genially pulling somebody's leg and he did this very amusingly by propounding a comic mathematical problem to a non-mathematical mind" (Cohen *Interviews* 67). Children, especially, enjoyed his teasing and pranks.

One of his students recalled that "at the dinner table he liked to 'quiz' his neighbors with occasional conundrums with a mathematical air, which I at any rate found very entertaining" (Cohen *Interviews* 66). In the Alice books, he uses the language of nonsense.

One of the first lessons we learn from reading the nonsense in the Alice books is that language does not always carry meaning. The most famous example of this is the poem "Jabberwocky," which doubly resists meaning. First, the poem resists interpretation because of the way it appears in mirror-fashion. This mirror prose is reminiscent of da Vinci's mirror-writing in his diaries (he also had traits of AS), and we know that many people with autism are dyslexic, reading things in reverse. The poem also resists interpretation because it is written in a nonsense version of English. The grammar structure feels "English-y," but the vocabulary is baffling:

> 'Twas brillig, and the slithy toves
> Did gyre and gimble in the wabe:
> All mimsy were the borogoves,
> And the mome raths outgrabe… (134)

After reading the poem, Alice tries to figure out what it means: "It seems very pretty," she concludes, "but it's *rather* hard to understand." Through this poem, Carroll shows us that language does not always carry meaning—but sometimes we can enjoy it just for the way it sounds. Years later, Gertrude Stein and James Joyce would carry this concept to the extreme, as would "abstract expressionist" poets.

In the "Lobster Quadrille" chapter of *AAW*, the Gryphon tells Alice to recite "'Tis the Voice of the Sluggard," a didactic 18th century poem taught to Victorian children. But when Alice opens her mouth, another poem comes tumbling out: "'Tis the Voice of the Lobster," a nonsense poem that was *not* written for the edification of *anyone*. Like "Jabberwocky," this poem carries little meaning. Upon hearing it, the Mock Turtle is puzzled: "Well, I never heard it before," he says, "but it sounds uncommon nonsense." It also sounds like a lot of fun.

Humpty Dumpty carries on a nonsensical conversation with Alice that feels like a badminton game. Ironically, what makes this conversation so silly and strange is the strictly literal meaning he gives to each spoken phrase:

> "So here's a question for you. How old did you say you were?"
>
> Alice made a short calculation, and said, "Seven years and six months."
>
> "Wrong!" Humpty Dumpty exclaimed triumphantly. "You never said a word like it!"
>
> "I thought you meant, 'How old *are* you?'" Alice explained.
>
> "If I'd meant that, I'd have said it," said Humpty Dumpty. (188)

Literal speech like this is a trait shared by other AS individuals. A little bit further, Humpty Dumpty teaches Alice that words are slippery and can't easily be pinned down. In this scene, he is selling Alice on the idea that un-birthday presents are better than birthday presents since she can collect so many more of them. He closes his argument by saying, "And only *one* [day] for birthday presents you know. There's glory for you." When Alice asks him what he means by "there's glory for you," he tells her that it means "there's a nice knock-down argument for you." This leads him to his pet theory on language: when he uses a word, it means exactly what *he* wants it to mean, neither more nor less. Cohen reminds us that "Wonderland and the world behind the looking-glass are mysterious places where characters do not live by conventional rules and where meaning does not play a conventional role" (*Biography* 142).

Lewis Carroll is doing nothing here if not showing off his linguistic and logical acumen with Aspergen aplomb. He is like Alice, who enjoys "showing off her knowledge." This book is a series of games for him: a game he can always win. How does he gain extra points? By showing off and using language that does double-duty: puns, parody, satire, and acrostics. The puns are especially fun, for they bring us the alternative interpretation that Wonderland is symbolic of school: where you can learn about reeling and writhing; or study the arithmetical branches of ambition, distraction, uglification, and derision; and don't forget mystery or drawling; or those old classics Laughing and Grief. Remembering that he wrote these books for children puts this nonsensical humor into perspective: he could relate to children better than he could relate to adults, and the humor in this book is nothing if not silly and childish. "He is a genius at double meanings, at playing games with words, and he challenges every child who picks up the book to play the game with him. And when the child catches Charles's second meaning…the child has played the game right and can share a private joke with the author" (Cohen *Biography* 143).

Conclusion

Even though Carroll himself would never have admitted this, in writing the Alice books he gave his readers the opportunity to get a small glimpse into the man himself. I agree with his biographer that studying this book is the key to understanding Carroll's emotional history:

> The Alice books become, in this metaphor, a record of Charles's childhood, the shocks dealt him by parents, teachers, all his elders. Bad manners and violence were commonplace in Victorian days, but their emphasis and frequency in these books, while capturing the ethos of the age, also tell us that Charles must have stored up an amount of hostility as he grew up, at home, at school, and at Oxford. At home and at school, he very likely smarted under innumerable commands from above, unreasoning and unreasonable, and as a sensitive observer, he saw and deplored society's artificial and meaningless minuets. The spare-the-rod philosophy was still dominant; whippings and beatings at school were customary. The bullying he

> witnessed, the knockabout games on the sporting fields, surely weighed on him. Accumulated resentment seeks outlets, and Charles took this opportunity [writing the *Alice* books] to get even with the past. (Cohen *Biography* 139)

If one reads the *Alice* books sympathetically, it is possible to see the frustration, confusion, and unhappiness that must have filled his life. Growing up is hard enough, but growing up with AS is doubly hard.

But was his childhood entirely bleak? No. As the *Alice* books reveal to us, his life was also filled with laughter, with jokes, and with fun. And, in writing these books, he gave himself the opportunity to show off his wit, his intelligence, and his superior handling of language. In his books he seems to say, "I celebrate myself and sing myself." If the *Alice* books do reflect the chaotic, confusing issues associated with an AS childhood, they also offer up an antidote: the playground of the mind, complete with intellectual gymnastics, linguistic games, and a good dose of humorous nonsense. Just as these pursuits gave him pleasure in life, they also added richness, vitality, and originality to his two greatest works. Lewis Carroll's Asperger's Syndrome was both the illness and the medicine to cure it.

Works Cited

Blastland, Michael. *The Only Boy in the World: A Father Explores the Mysteries of Autism.* New York: Marlowe & Company, 2006.

Carroll, Lewis. *Alice's Adventures in Wonderland and Through the Looking-Glass.* Oxford: Oxford University Press, 1971. All quotations taken from this edition.

Cohen, Martin, ed. *The Letters of Lewis Carroll.* New York: Oxford University Press, 1979.

Cohen, Martin. *Lewis Carroll: A Biography.* New York: Vintage, 1995.

---. *Lewis Carroll: Interviews and Recollections.* Iowa City: University of Iowa Press, 1989.

Fitzgerald, Michael. *Autism and Creativity: Is There a Link between Autism in Men and Exceptional Ability?* New York: Brunner-Routledge, 2004.

---. *The Genesis of Artistic Creativity: Asperger's Syndrome and the Arts.* London: Jessica Kingsley Publishers, 2005.

---. *Unstoppable Brilliance: Irish Geniuses and Asperger's Syndrome.* Dublin: Liberties Press, 2006.

Heffner, Gary. "Echolalia and Autism." The Autism Home Page. http://sites.google.com/site/autismhome/Home/special-situations/echolalia

Holliday Willey, Lianne. *Pretending to Be Normal: Living with Asperger's Syndrome.* London: Jessica Kingsley Publishers, 1999.

Rimland, Bernard. Introduction to *Nobody Nowhere* by Donna Williams. New York: Avon, 1992.

Williams, Donna. *Nobody Nowhere: The Extraordinary Autobiography of an Autistic.* New York: Avon, 1992.

CHAPTER SEVEN

William Butler Yeats

It would be hard to think of a writer more brilliant, more accomplished, or more honored than the Irish poet William Butler Yeats (1865–1939). He started writing while in his teens, and rapidly developed his talent while he was still a young man in his twenties. His first book-length poem, *The Wanderings of Oisin,* was published when he was just 23, and two more volumes, *Crossways* and *The Rose,* appeared before his thirtieth birthday. He remained a prolific writer throughout his life—even as an old man in his seventies he continued writing poems at a breathless pace. His early poems demonstrate a fine Victorian sense of rhythm, rhyme, and image; but his later works, with a heavier emphasis on symbol, ambiguity, and cynicism, establish him as one of the great modernist poets. His poems speak of themes important to himself, to Ireland, and to all of humanity. In 1923 he was awarded the Nobel Prize for "his always inspired poetry, which in a highly artistic form gives expression to the spirit of a whole nation" (Nobelprize.org). Today his poetry is loved for "its lyricism, its simple beauty and symbolism, and its profound love of Irish myth and landscape" (Fitzgerald *Brilliance* x).

Yeats and Asperger's Syndrome

To those Yeats fans who are familiar with his poetry but not with the details of his life story, it might come as a surprise that Yeats exhibited signs of Asperger's Syndrome (AS). In his research, Michael Fitzgerald has outlined the numerous behaviors of Yeats that place him on the autistic spectrum, concluding that "a diagnosis of Asperger's Syndrome certainly comes close to bridging the excesses and eccentricities of his personality and his creative genius" (*Brilliance* 218). He suffered from social impairments, communication problems, sensory issues, and fixations. As we shall see, these AS traits contributed to his unique poetic genius.

Much of Yeats's early years were passed in Sligo, at the rambling country home of his maternal grandparents, where he first began to demonstrate traits of Asperger's Syndrome. Yeats preferred chasing dogs through the woods to playing with other children. He was withdrawn and shy and seemed to be in his own little world much of the time. He had poor vision, asymmetrical eyes, and he had an "odd gait" that was so peculiar his grandmother tried to teach him how to walk without "stumping [his] heels" (Yeats 14). He was hopelessly awkward at sports. He could neither read nor write by age nine and his family thought he was retarded.

Like Lewis Carroll, Yeats's most miserable years were spent at school, where his AS differences set him apart from the others. At an English school he did not mix well with the other boys, who picked on him continually and called him "the mad Irishman." Yeats remembered, "I had a harassed life and got many a black eye and had many outbursts of grief and rage" (Yeats 22). Like Thoreau, Yeats preferred to roam about in nature by himself. In need of both rigorous physical exercise and also time away from other people, he would walk for miles, alone, and curl up at night to sleep in caves and under gigantic rhododendron bushes. During this time, his father often read poetry and other literary texts to him, and Yeats was inspired to take up his own pen.

Though the symptoms of AS became more manageable as he grew older, he was still awkward in social situations and still had more than his share of "blunders." For example, soon after joining the Theosophist Society, he was asked to resign for asking too many questions. At a dinner party for distinguished writers, he gave the man sitting next to him a list of reasons why he disliked T. S. Eliot's poetry—not realizing that it was Eliot he was speaking to. When he heard that friend and playwright J. M. Synge was ill, he shocked those around him when he publicly shouted the bizarre remark, "I hope he will die" (Yeats 345). Yeats felt that he behaved unnaturally, that he suffered from a "tendency to pose" (Yeats 318). He was often miserable: "I cry constantly against my life," he wrote in his autobiography, wishing somehow to become a "normal, active man" (Yeats 333).

As an adult, Yeats pursued several inappropriate love interests, including one married woman, one daughter of a friend, and his most famous one-sided love for Maud Gonne. By the time he was 52, he decided it was time to get serious about passing on the family name (plus his horoscope said he needed to get married—fast). In marrying Georgie Hyde-Lees (he called her "George"), he actually made the best possible choice. He was drawn to her because she was young and pretty, but her other qualities proved to be even more important. She believed in his poetic genius, and did everything she could to help further his career. She took care of him in a motherly way, making sure he ate right, got enough sleep, and buttoned up his shirts the right way. She gave him what he had never had before: unconditional love, security, comfort, and a family of his own. Within four years they had two children, Anne and Michael. Fitzgerald notes, "Without a doubt Yeats had the good fortune to marry her...she was the perfect mother figure for him, aside from being his muse...his wife organized him and devoted herself to helping him express his creativity" (Fitzgerald *Autism* 180). Many Yeats biographers credit her for helping him to emerge from his "isolation and eccentricity." Fitzgerald believes that "had he remained a bachelor, it is unlikely that he would have become the Nobel Laureate celebrated today" (*Autism* 189).

The key to understanding Yeats's poetry is the influence of his autism on his life and his writing. His place on the spectrum gave him a gift for rich language and musical sound, an intense interest in Irish folklore that provided him with subject matter, and a profound talent for communicating through symbol.

An Oral/Kinetic Writing Process

In the case of creative geniuses, an intense, Aspergen focus allows an artist to give complete attention to the project at hand while blocking out the rest of the world and its distractions. Yeats was like this with his poetry. As a young man writing at home, he could scribble out poems and chant out the lines in a small room while five other family members shared the single lamp with him.

It was necessary for him to say the lines aloud, repeating them with variation until he found the one that sounded right. Fitzgerald points out that "Repetition features prominently in Yeats' use of language…John Yeats noticed how his boy liked an appealing or resonant phrase, which, once heard, he would repeat over and over again" (*Brilliance* 223). This tendency is related to the autistic echolalia of some individuals on the spectrum. Harold Bloom finds great power and majesty in Yeats's intuitive use of repetition: "The genius of refrain never abandoned Yeats" (769).

His writing process was also tied to his finely developed hearing, which tuned him into the beauty of sound. After recording Yeats reading his work, BBC producer George Barnes remarked "how strange it was that Yeats was utterly tone-deaf to music, yet his ear for sound was sensitive beyond belief and picked up nuances of intonation that others could hardly hear" (Maddox 334).

He was a kinetic writer who often composed poetry while walking (Thoreau also wrote while walking, and Carroll rowed a boat while telling the first Alice story), and he would walk the streets of Dublin, simultaneously chanting lines and flapping his arms wildly up and down like a seagull to the point where the local police became concerned. They weren't sure what to make of the mad man flapping and walking and chanting, until someone informed them that the young man was a poet. This explanation satisfied them. When Yeats was working on a poem, the rest of the world ceased to exist. It's lucky for Yeats—and for all of us—that he found a wife who could support and nurture this bizarre kind of genius. He wrote some of his greatest works while married to Georgie, and she was careful to give him the uninterrupted time and emotional stability he needed to focus on his work.

Language/Sound

Many people on the autistic spectrum process sensory information in a way that either dulls or sharpens one particular sense. A heightened awareness of sound, color, texture, or light contributes greatly to the power of their work. In Yeats's case, he suffered from visual problems but had especially acute hearing, like Thoreau and Emily Dickinson. His ear was sensitive to linguistic sounds, and he had an uncanny ability to shape the language of his poetry into lyrical melody. Some of his most beautiful lines, and certainly the most famous, gain strength through a rhythmic chanting of mesmerizing syllables: "his is the poetry of refrain, of repetition in a finer tone, raised to the Sublime, at the limits of art" (Bloom 769).

Yeats's earlier poems reflect a traditional approach to writing poetry with regular stanzas that feature a predictable rhythm pattern, a regular rhyme scheme, repetition of words, lines, or stanzas, and a good dose of alliteration. Consider these stanzas from an early poem, written by Yeats when he was 24:

> Shy one, shy one,
> Shy one of my heart,
> She moves in the firelight
> Pensively apart
>
> She carries in the dishes
> And lays them in a row
> To an isle in the water
> With her I would go

She carries in the candles,
And lights the curtained room,
Shy in the doorway
And shy in the gloom;

And shy as a rabbit,
Helpful and shy.
To an isle in the water
With her I would fly. (54)

The "chanting" quality of this poem seems to be linked to Yeats's oral and kinetic writing process. The music of his rhythm and rhyme, as well as the extensive use of alliteration, is no doubt influenced by Yeats's fine hearing sense. The repetition of words and phrases has a strong echolalic feel to it—many writers with AS rely on repetition for building up the sound and adding layers to the meaning.

Later on in his life, Yeats was to become part of the modernist movement that made "free verse" poetry its centerpiece, and even though over time his poetry had a less structured rhyme and rhythm pattern, he still filled his poetry with music. Consider these lines from "The Second Coming" (1919, 294), one of the most important poems of all time:

Turning and turning in the widening gyre (repetition)
The falcon cannot hear the falconer; (repetition)
Things fall apart; the centre cannot hold; (strong rhythm)
Mere anarchy is loosed upon the world, (strong rhythm)
The blood-dimmed tide is loosed, and everywhere (repetition, alliteration)
The ceremony of innocence is drowned; (alliteration)
The best lack all conviction, while the worst (alliteration)
Are full of passionate intensity. (strong rhythm)

Even though the rhythm pattern is not predictable, the variation of stresses on the syllables creates tension and strength. And even though there is no predictable rhyme pattern, certain sound patterns are echoed ("turn," "gyre," "world," "worst") in a pleasing way. The use of repetition in this poem contributes to its apocryphal feeling. Even though readers have been scratching their heads for years over the exact meaning of this poem, when this poem is read out loud, the strength and impact of Yeats's poetics contribute greatly to the overall message of fear and dread.

Yeats took on the air of a conjurer when he prepared to write a poem. His son Michael recalled:

> All the family knew the signs, we were careful to do nothing that might interrupt the flow of thought. Without warning he would begin to make a low, tuneless humming sound, and his right hand would wave vaguely as if beating time. This could happen at the dinner table, while playing croquet, or sitting in a bus, and he would become totally oblivious to what was going on around him. (Fitzgerald *Genesis* 76)

He was something of a magician with language—he knew the mesmerizing power that certain kinds of sounds and phrases could have on his audience. When reading his poems aloud, he seemed to cast a spell on himself and those within hearing range—even now, one may listen to a recording of Yeats reading his poetry and fall under its hypnotic sway. Yeats's rich and powerful poetics were greatly influenced by his Asperger's Syndrome.

Characterization: An Interest in Fairies

Yeats's writing, both his poetry and his prose, features numerous references to fairies. Fairies reflect the tendency of AS writers to present characters that are flashy and have an interesting physical presence, but are not emotionally or intellectually developed. Yeats's interest in writing about fairies is similar to Hans Christian

Andersen's interest in mermaids and emperors or Lewis Carroll's comic book citizens of Wonderland.

Yeats had been introduced to fairies while staying with his grandparents in Sligo. Both family and servants frequently told tales of otherworldly creatures, and his mother Susan especially relished these stories, as Yeats recalled: she "liked best of all to exchange ghost and fairy stories with some fisherman's wife in the kitchen" (Ellman 24). As a child, Yeats definitely believed in fairies, recalling in his memoirs how they would ride to him on a moonbeam, "whisper in his ear," and even play pranks on him. Throughout his life, Yeats associated western Ireland with fairies. "The Stolen Child" shows us Yeats's fascination for fairy folk.

In this poem, a tribe of fairies lives on an island in a lake. Their homeland is a natural paradise with leafy trees and juicy berries. The fairies decide to lure a "normal" child to their island, offering him a reprieve from the sorrows of civilization. This refrain is repeated several times in the poem:

> Come away, O human child!
> To the waters and the wild
> With a faery hand in hand
> For the world's more full of weeping than you can
> understand.

The child follows the fairies, and he is enamored by the midnight rituals of these strange, magical beings:

> We foot it all the night,
> Weaving olden dances,
> Mingling hands and mingling glances
> Till the moon has taken flight

In the end the child decides to join the fairy society, though it means leaving behind the comforts of home, such as a hot bowl of porridge or a comforting fire. For reasons that are not explained, he chooses to join a group of alien beings rather than stay with his own people. The fairies become his new tribe. Their island provides him with both safety from the outside world and also the society of kindred spirits. This need to leave home in order to join others parallels the yearnings that many AS people have to strike out and find others who are like them. One can imagine young Yeats, camping in the woods, dreaming of the fairy folk that he might someday like to join: folk who are different from others of the world, just like him.

Yeats wrote about fairies throughout his life, both in his poetry and also in his writings about Irish folklore and culture. This interest in "fairy folk" seems to be common in people with AS. Other AS writers such as Hans Christian Andersen, Lewis Carroll, and Opal Whiteley were also interested in fairies and wrote about them. Today, AS individuals are often drawn to characters from fantasy (Dungeons and Dragons games), mythology (computerized role-playing games such as Age of Mythology), and science fiction (Star Trek, Star Wars), not to mention the current obsession with Japanese Anime (cartoons) and Manga (comic books). What fantastic characters such as fairies, Greek gods, aliens, and so on all have in common are the very reasons why AS people find them appealing: they are simple and uncomplicated, lacking the emotional complexity of humans; they are easily categorized by type, which adds to the Aspergen pleasure of identifying and classifying and sorting and collecting them; and they have heightened sensory ability and special magic powers which make them very attractive. In early adulthood, Yeats was fascinated by fairies for all of these reasons. Later on, he showed a similar preoccupation with "avatars" from the spirit realm.

Yeats's fixation on fairies is interesting in another way as well. Carole G. Silver's recent study, *Strange and Secret Peoples*, explores the relationship between creatures of folklore and humans with birth defects, arguing that, centuries ago, babies who were born with abnormal physical or mental development were assumed to be "changelings." Several scholars have recently pointed to the changeling myth as being one explanation for how a baby with autism could be brought to a typical household—the "real baby" is taken away by the fairies, and a "defective substitute" is left behind in its place. As an adult, Yeats studied Irish folklore and collected folk stories for publication in his book *Celtic Twilight*. He was particularly fascinated with the stories of changelings. In an unpublished manuscript about fairies, he warned in all seriousness that "All the young are in danger [from fairy kidnapping]" (Silver 71). He based this theory on the supposition that "Fairies needed mortals for their physical strength" (Silver 74). In his notes for this poem, Yeats also mentions that near Rosses Point (where "The Stolen Child" is set), for anyone who falls asleep, "there is a danger of their waking silly, the faeries having carried off their souls." It is interesting to speculate as to whether Yeats ever felt himself to be a changeling, especially when he was a child. One could certainly imagine his father shaking his head at young Willie, wondering where this strange child came from.

Personal Symbols of Autism

As Yeats yearned to understand who he was and what he was destined to become, he used writing as a tool for self discovery. Biographer Richard Ellman notes: "he spent much of his life attempting to understand the deep contradictions within his mind," and turned to writing to resolve the "ultimate perplexity as to the meaning of his experiences" (4). He poured his heart into diaries, letters, poems, and other manuscripts, and the central topic of all his writings was his quest to understand himself.

For every poem he wrote was, in a sense, a fragmented piece of himself. As he wrote in a letter to his friend Katherine Tynan: "My life has been in my poems. To make them I have broken my life in a mortar as it were" (Ellman 54). Yet rather than directly addressing the concerns of his life, he cloaked each one in symbol. Partly, this was due to the Romantic tradition he was working in. But Yeats also noted that he preferred to communicate symbolically rather than directly: "A poet writes of his personal life, in his finest work out of its tragedy, whatever it be, remorse, lost love, loneliness; he never speaks directly as to someone at the breakfast table, there is always a phantasmagoria [symbolic presentation]" (Bloom 64). This use of symbolism was the best way for a shy writer on the spectrum to explore his feelings without directly exposing them. Yeats developed two images, the island and the tower, that can be read as personal symbols for his autism.

Other writers with autism have constructed personal symbols that represent their autism and their feelings toward it. In Temple Grandin's autobiography, she develops the symbol of the "door" and shows how a door can either block her forward progress or open up and allow her through. In Donna Williams' poetry, she uses the image of the mirror to represent the world "in here" and the world "out there." Writer and mathematician Daniel Tammet is fascinated by prime numbers, but identifies most strongly with Pi, the powerful and unique number that never develops a pattern. It is enlightening to view Yeats's personal symbols in light of the emerging canon of autistic literature: Yeats's place on the spectrum was symbolically rendered through his poetry.

The Island: Isolation and Solitude

One of Yeats's most famous poems is "The Lake Isle of Innisfree" (74), which shows Yeats's feelings of "apartness" from other people. At the time that he wrote this poem he was living in London, and Innisfree ("island of heather"), the lake island near Sligo, was on his mind as a place of refuge and serenity, things he sorely missed when he lived in the busy, crowded city of London. In his autobiography he noted:

> I still had the ambition, formed in Sligo in my teens, of living in imitation of Thoreau on Innisfree, a little island in Lough Gill, and when walking through Fleet Street very homesick

> I heard a little tinkle of water...and began to remember lake water. From the sudden remembrance came my poem Innisfree, my first lyric with anything in its rhythm of my own music. (Yeats 103)

This epiphany was of great value to Yeats. For here he recognized how powerful the symbol of the island was for him as an individual, and would become for him as a poet.

In "Lake Isle of Innisfree" (written as a young man), Yeats says he will "arise and go now" to "Innisfree" and "a small cabin will [he] build there." He will plant beans, as Thoreau did, and gather honey from the "bee-loud glade." He will create a world of his own there; will be content to listen to the music of bees, crickets, and linnets. The repetitive sound of water lapping on the shore will soothe him. The island will provide a refuge from both "roadway" and "pavement," symbols of civilization. The final stanza reinforces the feeling of peaceful solitude:

> I will arise and go now, for always night and day
> I hear lake water lapping with low sounds by the shore;
> While I stand on the roadway, or on the pavements grey,
> I hear it in the deep heart's core.

The island will ask nothing of him. It will provide him with comfort and peace. In this case, the island represents the autistic solitude that he preferred. The water that surrounds it provides a boundary, a buffer zone, a margin between himself and other people, other islands, or continents. Many people on the autistic spectrum, overwhelmed by too much society and too much sensory overload, often prefer to be alone. I recently checked a discussion forum for people with Asperger's Syndrome, and when someone posted the question, "what do you like to do to relax?" nearly every respondent replied, "to be alone and hang out by myself" (www.aspiesforfreedom.com).

In "The Sad Shepherd" (42) also written in young adulthood, the island metaphor is expanded to represent the isolation that can be enforced upon one who is shunned by others. The shepherd walks along the shoreline, seeking a friend, but he finds that the others are all turning away from him. First he looks up, and beseeches the stars to befriend him. They deny him comfort:

> … He called loudly to the stars to bend
> From their pale thrones and comfort him, but they
> Among themselves laugh on and sing always

Rejected by the stars, he reaches out to the sea. The sea, too, rejects him:

> … *Dim sea, hear my most piteous story!*
> The sea swept on and cried her old cry still,
> Rolling along in dreams from hill to hill.

He finally turns inward toward the land, and desperately asks the egotistical dewdrops to hear his story, but they, too, refuse to listen:

> But naught they heard, for they are always listening,
> The dewdrops, for the sound of their own dropping.

Rejected by everyone around him, the sad shepherd finds that only "Sorrow" will be his friend. Eventually he decides to tell his own story into a shell, where the words will echo and re-echo sadly into the shell's heart.

Unlike Innisfree, this island is not a happy place for the hero. It is a place of rejection. Of separation from the tribe. Of desperately reaching out for friendship, and feeling miserable when the friendship is not returned. These feelings are familiar to many people with AS—they often suffer from anxiety and depression because of their social difficulties. Thus, "Sorrow" will name itself the shepherd's friend, as it did for young Yeats when he was a schoolboy in London and an adolescent in Dublin.

The final image of the voice echoing in the shell is an interesting choice. Yeats was somewhat echolalic as a child and in this poem the voice echoes endlessly in the chambers of a shell. The shepherd, like the poet, is speaking only to himself, babbling "till [his] own words, re-echoing, shall send/Their sadness through a hollow, pearly heart." In many of Yeats's poems, he repeats key lines in a refrain. Here in this poem, the repeated words dissolve into moaning. When language fails him, all he's left with is an inarticulate cry.

The Tower Symbol Emerges

The autistic island disappears as both an image and a symbol in his later poems. The island is replaced by the tower, the symbol that represents his autism from a more mature perspective. Unlike the island, the tower represents a position of strength, protection, and power. The island comes from mythology; the tower from history. The island is populated with fairies; the tower with great people. On the island, Yeats is often alone. In the tower, he keeps company with wife and children.

Several months after he married Georgie he took her to visit Sligo. According to local gossip, he rowed her out in the lake to show her Innisfree, but couldn't find it (Maddox 125). But what he could show her was Thoor Ballylee, a medieval tower, the first house he had ever purchased. They were both enchanted by the medieval architecture, the rich history, and the isolation of the place—Yeats was eager to make the tower into a home for himself and his young bride. The tower was to replace the island as the symbol for his sense of himself. Yeats wrote this little poem to commemorate the place:

To be Carved on a Stone at Thoor Ballylee

I, the poet William Yeats,
With old mill boards and sea-green slates,

And smithy work from the Gort forge,
Restored this tower for my wife George;
And may these characters remain
When all is ruin once again. (298)

The tower, like Yeats, is old, and in need of restoration. But both welcome the new bride. After years pass, perhaps, both will fall to ruin once again. But for now, this is a cheerful time. Yeats has found a new symbol for self: "I claim this tower is my symbol," he wrote. Yeats has abandoned the island for the tower. Significantly, this is the first time Yeats calls himself by his own name in a poem.

One of the first poems he wrote in the tower was "A Prayer for my Daughter," written after the birth of Anne Butler Yeats in 1919. The tower figures prominently in this poem, both as setting and symbol. Yeats and his daughter huddle indoors while a wild, dangerous storm is screaming outside. The storm is "roof-levelling," and "howling," and the nearby stream is "flooded." The outer world is a dangerous, violent, frightening place. The storm symbolism here is clearly linked to the political situation in Ireland. The last few years had seen the Easter Sunday uprising, the revolution against England, and the execution of Irish nationalists. World War I had recently ended, and Irish men had been conscripted to fight for England.

But Yeats and his daughter are safe inside. The thick stone walls provide both insulation from the storm and isolation from the world. The quiet space within gives Yeats the chance to meditate and to pray for his daughter. Though he feels his own mind "has dried up of late," he asks for simple gifts for her, and these gifts reveal both his tender love for his child and also his final, complete understanding of what brings happiness: simple beauty, kindness, friendship, and innocence. His final wish is that she will marry, and that her bridegroom will take her to a house of her own. His own "homecoming" has been the culmination of his own happiness, and he wishes the same for Anne.

Comparing this poem directly to "Innisfree" reveals a continued desire for separation from the outside world, and a continued search for peace. But there are important differences. In the tower he is no longer alone: he has the company of a daughter he loves, as well as the responsibility of raising her, and he has learned to put someone else's needs ahead of his own. Furthermore, the fact that he can father a child at age 54 proves that he is no longer a fumbling adolescent but now is a sexually potent man (he feared impotence throughout his life), deserving of his phallic tower—which Ezra Pound nicknamed "Ballyphallus" (Maddox 264).

Yeats wrote several poems featuring tower imagery, and was to turn his thoughts to the tower one last time a few days before he died in 1939. In "The Black Tower" (455), a group of old Celtic warriors is holed up in a tower, awaiting the return of their king after a battle. A nearby grave holds the bones of their fallen comrades, who are buried upright in the ancient tradition. The warriors are hungry, tired, and defeated, but still they loyally wait for the king who may never rejoin them. The fragmented poem seems to end without an ending. We never learn whether or not the old king shows up to resume his leadership. The closing reference only repeats the refrain of the bones of the dead:

> There in the tomb the dark grows blacker,
> But wind comes up from the shore:
> They shake when the winds roar,
> Old bones upon the mountain shake.

Like all of Yeats's great works, this poem is rich with symbolic meaning and may be read in several ways. The immediate story comes from Celtic legend, of course. According to biographer R. F. Foster, the poem refers to a play Yeats had seen in Dublin 30 years earlier, produced by Patrick Pearse, which told the story of "remnants of Fianna brotherhood hiding in poverty, clinging to the resolution that their king will return" (648). The sight of the battered warriors clinging to their dream of victory stirred Yeats, calling to mind the recent struggles for Irish independence. After he had seen the play, Yeats wrote to Lady Gregory expressing his impression that "the waiting of old men of the defeated clan seemed so like ourselves" (Foster 648).

But Yeats's poem, written in 1939 as Europe was entering another bloody Armageddon, was clearly also a reaction to the present times. He was in France when he wrote this, and everyone was fearful about the German machine right across the border. Yeats believed that time and history were cyclical, and that historical meaning spiraled and repeated itself in layers. As World War II followed so close on the heels of World War I, the spiral was quickly tightening. Georgie referred to the poem as "political propaganda."

But a re-examination of the poem in terms of Yeats's earlier uses of the tower as a symbol of himself gives way to a final glimpse of Yeats as a man on the autistic spectrum. "The Black Tower" is not a hopeful poem, as the previous tower poems had been. There is no longer a feeling of warmth or well-being within. No wives or children reside here to give the men comfort. The food supply is dwindling and the men do not even hunt for deer—they "feed as the goatherd feeds" on small animals they can snare.

Approaching banners suggest that the enemy draws near as the men wait hopelessly for their leader to return. Is this perhaps Yeats's final acknowledgement of despair at his own situation? That in the end the world "whispers that a man's a fool" for believing in himself, his abilities, his value as an individual? For all the glories Yeats had won—including the Nobel Prize—he still questioned his worthiness as a human being. He *knew* his friends mocked and ridiculed him behind his back. People who knew him well joked often about his sexual difficulties, his obsession with the occult, his poor social skills, and his lack of sensitivity—all of these were challenges that stemmed from his AS and could not be helped. Yeats may have felt a little like Andersen's emperor with no clothes—foolishly believing in his idea of himself when everyone else could see the embarrassing truth.

Conclusion

Even though Yeats said throughout his life "I know very little about myself" (115), he did understand that something about him was different and that this difference caused his isolation and separateness from the world. And what he did know of himself he etched into his poems: "I…write many poems where an always personal emotion [is] woven into a general pattern of myth and symbol" (Yeats 102). By paying close attention to his poetic writing style, we can learn a great deal about how a person's neurology affects the way that he uses language. By paying close attention to his emphasis on fairies, we can learn a great deal about what fascinates the mind of an individual who is on the autism spectrum. And by paying close attention to his construction of island and tower symbolism, we can learn a great deal about how this poetic genius felt about himself and his place in the world.

Works Cited

Bloom, Harold. *Yeats.* Oxford: Oxford University Press, 1970.

Ellman, Richard. *Yeats: The Man and the Masks.* New York: Norton, 1978.

Fitzgerald, Michael. *Autism and Creativity.* New York: Taylor and Francis, 2004.

---. *The Genesis of Artistic Creativity: Asperger's Syndrome and the Arts.* London: Jessica Kingsley Publishers, 2005.

Fitzgerald, Michael and Antoinette Walker. *Unstoppable Brilliance: Irish Geniuses and Asperger's Syndrome.* Dublin: Liberties Press, 2006.

Foster, R. F. *W. B. Yeats: A Life.* Oxford: Oxford University Press, 2003.

Jeffares, A. Norman, ed. *Yeats's Poems* (An anthology of Yeats's poems and extensive commentary by Jeffares). Dublin: Gill and Macmillan, 1989. All quotations from Yeats's poems are taken from this edition.

Maddox, Brenda. *Yeats's Ghosts.* New York: HarperCollins, 1999.

Silver, Carol G. *Strange and Secret Peoples.* Oxford: Oxford University Press, 1999.

Yeats, William Butler. *The Autobiography of William Butler Yeats.* New York: Collier, 1965.

CHAPTER EIGHT

Sherwood Anderson

Family Background and Asperger's Syndrome

American author Sherwood Anderson (1876–1941) wrote many books during his lifetime—over a dozen novels, several memoirs, and short story collections, including his most important literary achievement, *Winesburg, Ohio.* He grew up in a small Midwestern town and came from a family of eccentrics that always skirted the edges of society. His father was unable to run a successful business, the family was always short of money, and the mother was forced to take in laundry in order to put food on the table. Anderson started working odd jobs as a child, earning the nickname "Jobby" for his willingness to deliver newspapers and to help out in the small town businesses. Anderson left school at 14 for manual labor jobs and a stint in the military.

After attending college he married, had three children, and discovered that he could write. The struggle between responsibility (family, business, community) and freedom (travel, writing, art) was difficult for him to manage, and the stress of it led to several nervous breakdowns. After his fourth marriage, he finally found peace in a stone cabin in Virginia, where he edited two newspapers, one Democrat, one Republican.

Evidence suggests that Sherwood and several family members had traits of autism spectrum disorder. Anderson's father Irwin was a heavy drinker and a talker who would corner everyone, strangers and friends alike, and talk *at* them incessantly. His mother would fall into frustrating "deep silences" (Anderson *Storyteller* 9). The family never reached a position of status in the community and was not highly thought of. In order to learn more about this family, I traveled to Clyde, Ohio (where the Anderson boys grew up) to interview town historian Dorothy Cox. Cox personally knew people associated with the Andersons, and when I asked her about possible autism in the family, she immediately started to talk about Sherwood's younger brother Earl. The baby of the family, Earl displayed many traits of full-blown autism. He was the "strange one," she said, a loner who had no friends. The other kids in town teased him and called him "Stumblebum" because he didn't say much, and when he did try to talk, he stuttered and had speech problems. An uncontrollable nervous tic of rolling his tongue along the inside of his cheek turned people away. Cox related that he "stared through people" in an unnerving way, and said he "drove everyone crazy." He was close to his brother Sherwood but not to anyone else.

Sherwood demonstrated traits of Asperger's Syndrome. Growing up he was a dreamer, often lost in his own world, absorbed by his own thoughts. When called by name he didn't answer, even if someone was screaming at him. He was an avid reader who withdrew into a world of books. People recalled that Sherwood's eyes would glaze over and he couldn't always attend to what was being said. He made friends with other boys in town, but often confused them by his strange comments and odd behaviors, such as stomping on his brand new hat. His behavior was often impulsive.

As an adult at work in an advertising agency, he could often be found lost in his thoughts, staring out the office window. Although he was a talented writer who was good at creating ad copy, he relied on others to keep him organized. He depended upon his secretary to decipher his illegible handwriting and to correct his spelling and erratic punctuation. Socially, he fluctuated between being a "lone wolf" who sought isolation, and desperately needing an audience (just like Hans Christian Andersen, Yeats, and Lewis Carroll). In group conversations he often dominated the discussion and annoyed others by constantly talking of himself. He once noted that it took a "bracing effort" for him to make eye contact with others (Rideout V1 296; Anderson *Storyteller* 18), and it is possible that he suffered from *prosopagnosia*, or face blindness: in his memoirs Anderson confesses, "I do not know what my wife looks like. I cannot remember the face of my one sister, my mother's face, or the faces of any of my best known men friends and acquaintances" (*Memoirs* 159).

Several of his autistic traits, including his poor social skills, his communication problems, his inability to follow social conventions, and his feelings of alienation, contributed to the way that he wrote literature. In *Winesburg, Ohio,* Anderson created characters with Asperger's Syndrome who inhabited landscapes that symbolically represented isolation and alienation. Anderson's willingness to "go his own way" made it possible for him to create a new literary genre, the "novel in stories," which opened up a whole new way of telling a story. Additionally, his struggles with verbal communication no doubt contributed to his slippery, inexact language and descriptions—in this way he (along with his friend Gertrude Stein) helped shape the modernist dictum that language cannot represent reality. An examination of *Winesburg, Ohio*, including a close look at three of his stories, has a lot to teach us about the impact of Asperger's Syndrome on literary writing.

Winesburg, Ohio: A Book of Grotesques

Winesburg, Ohio is a collection of loosely related short stories set in a small town in Ohio. One thread that holds the collection together is the character of George Willard, a young man who, by virtue of his parents' owning a hotel and his job as reporter for the newspaper, seems to know almost everyone in town. In some ways George resembles Sherwood Anderson: his father is a talker and his mother is quiet; he comes of age in a small Ohio town that he eventually outgrows; he is good with written language, and he has dreams of becoming a writer. George doesn't have close friends his own age, but he does have informal friendships with many of the town's "grotesques," in relationships reminiscent of that between Sherwood and his brother Earl.

Anderson introduces us to this word in an opening prologue story, called "The Book of the Grotesque" (this was also the original title for the entire collection). In this story an old man, a writer, is lying in his bed thinking over his life. His thoughts are interrupted by a vision: he imagines that a parade of figures is walking through his room, a parade of people he has known throughout his life. But these figures are not normal: "They were all grotesques. All of the men and women the writer had ever known had become grotesques... Some were amusing, some almost beautiful, and one, a woman drawn all out of shape, hurt the old man by her grotesqueness" (4). In the prologue, the old writer thinks about what makes these people grotesque, and draws the conclusion that people become grotesque when they cling too obsessively to one single truth—whether it be the truth of virginity, or the truth of passion; the truth of wealth, or the truth of poverty; the truth of carelessness, or other truths. People become grotesque, he theorizes, when their adherence to one single truth makes them blind to everything else in their lives. His definition fits several traits of autism spectrum disorder: many of Anderson's grotesque characters display rigid thinking, narrow interests, perseveration, and obsession with special interests. As we shall see, many of the grotesques in this book resemble Sherwood's youngest brother Earl, and others resemble Sherwood himself.

The old man does not appear in the rest of the short stories, however, so George Willard takes his place as the observer of human nature. By watching and listening, George comes to a complex and profound understanding of how people become miserable and unattractive to others. George encounters a dozen characters in Winesburg who would be considered "grotesque" by the old man's definition; not surprisingly, these "outsiders" exhibit other traits of autism as well: impaired social skills (they cannot make or keep friends; are alienated from the town), impaired communication skills (they talk too much, too little, or say odd things), and physical problems (clumsiness, muteness, hand-flapping). Whereas the old man is interested in identifying and cataloguing these individuals, George takes another approach—he befriends them, spends time with them, and seeks to understand them, trying to become their friend. His attempt to view these individuals as human, rather than as grotesques, mirrors the compassion that Sherwood felt for his brother Earl.

In the short stories that comprise the rest of the book, Anderson presents one autistic character after another. Each one inhabits a landscape that is symbolic of their oddness and their isolation from the rest of society. In "Queer," "Loneliness," and "Hands," Anderson relates the message that a community should pull together to respect and accept each one of its members with gestures of friendship, even toward those who are disabled in some way.

The Short Stories: "Queer"

The short story "Queer" describes one such attempt at understanding and friendship. Elmer Cowley, son of a local merchant, desperately wants to fit in with the others in town. He is an outsider who yearns for a friend and yearns to be a respectable member of the community. But he knows he will always be seen as queer because of his odd ways and the odd ways of his family (like the Anderson family): Ebenezer, Elmer's father, wears the same ancient dirty coat, day after day; his father repeats odd phrases that make no sense to others; and his father can not properly administer either his farm or his small store. Elmer desperately wants to fit into the community, but can't because he, too, is odd: he can't lace his own shoes and wanders the store in stockinged feet; he can't converse with people who enter the store; and when he is excited his arms "pump up and down," his face moves "spasmodically," and he "[loses] control of his tongue" (242–243).

The family's outcast status is symbolized by their surroundings. Their store is shabby and run down, and is not on the main street, but on Maumee St., a less important side street. Voight's wagon shop is beside the store and noisy wagons pull in and out all day. Displayed in the store window are one enormous lump of coal and some ancient brown honeycombs, covered with dust. The widower Ebenezer and his two children sleep upstairs, not in a house in town. No one is interested in buying what they have to sell.

Elmer is miserable because he "had lived in Winesburg for a year and had made no friends. He was, he felt, one condemned to go through life without friends and he hated the thought" (235). When a vendor enters the store to show them a new product one day, Elmer believes his father is being tricked—Elmer waves a gun at the vendor, yelling "We ain't going to keep on being queer and have folks staring and listening" (232). He chases the vendor away and the vendor yells to the townspeople that Elmer's crazy, as if to humiliate him even further. Elmer lacks the social skills that would have been necessary to avoid or repair his own feelings of isolation and loneliness. By declaring a war against queerness, he has highlighted the very queerness he sought to eradicate. He seems doomed to being an outcast in an outcast family. He feels shame over his father's behavior, as Anderson had as a boy.

That evening, Elmer thinks of George Willard, a young man about his age who works in the newspaper office next door. Elmer is obsessed with George, who represents "normalcy" in Elmer's eyes. He approaches George in order to prove something to himself, to George, and to the town—that he isn't such a bad guy after all.

Elmer thinks if he can only get through to George, somehow convincing George that he is normal, then his position in the town will improve and he will be able to make friends. But once again, he lacks the conversation skills and social skills necessary to bring about the desired effect. And, once again, his behavior results in the exact opposite of what he hopes to achieve.

George is friendly toward Elmer. He is pleased to encounter Elmer in the street, thinking if nothing else maybe Elmer might give him a tip for a newspaper story. Elmer can't decide whether to approach or avoid George until one night when he wakes George up in the middle of the night and drags him to the train station. Elmer plans to provoke George in some way, to challenge George to accept him. But instead, standing at the train station late at night, his capacity for speech gives way, and he repeats his father's nonsense phrase to George: "I'll be washed and ironed. I'll be washed and ironed and starched" (243). George is so stunned he can't respond. Then, in the darkness of the train station in the middle of the night, Elmer pounds on George with both of his strong fists, sending George sprawling to unconscious oblivion. "I guess I showed him I ain't so queer," he mutters to himself, hopping a train to Cleveland.

Elmer's story develops a theme that runs throughout the book. Anderson's message to the reader is a sad one: many people in this world are born different and they can't easily change who they are or how they behave. Since they don't know how to fix their situation, they are shunned by others, and are destined to a life of loneliness and frustration. The alienation that Elmer and others feel is parallel to that felt by the five autistic autobiographers examined in the final chapter of this book. Knowing that something is wrong, but not knowing what the problem is or how to fix it, would be frustrating for anyone. Anderson makes this point in several of his *Winesburg* stories, and indeed it becomes one of the central themes of the book. These people are beyond the reach of everyone, even a caring, friendly person such as George Willard, someone who is willing to look beyond the "queerness" of their autism to the person inside. Even though it didn't work out, George did make the effort to befriend this lonely young man.

"Loneliness"

In "Loneliness," young Enoch Robinson (another "E" name, like Earl and Elmer) is another frustrated, lonely outsider who cannot fix his situation. Enoch grows up in a farmhouse on the outskirts of

Winesburg, in a structure that establishes an outsider status for the family. He and his mother live "two miles beyond the town limits. The farmhouse was painted brown and the blinds to all of the windows facing the road were kept closed…a flock of chickens… lay in the deep dust" (197).

Enoch resembles Sherwood and Earl even more closely than Elmer did. As a child, Enoch could be found walking down the middle of a road, completely lost in a book he was reading, and he was oblivious when others shouted his name (like Sherwood). As a youth he was quiet, "inclined to silence," and wanted to become an artist (like Earl). Enoch moves to New York City, where he lives alone in an oddly-shaped upstairs apartment. The "odd shape" of the apartment serves to emphasize Enoch's oddness. Enoch attends art school for a while and dreams of becoming an artist, but his quest for artistic achievement is tempered by a dose of realism: like Sherwood, Enoch marries, has children, and works for an advertising agency.

As the title suggests, Enoch is plagued by loneliness. He forms no attachments with others growing up in Winesburg, yet in New York he is able to meet a few people. He entertains groups of artists in his apartment for superficial "art talk," but even in the crowd, Enoch is apart from the others:

> …these people gathered and smoked cigarettes and talked and Enoch Robinson, the boy from the farm near Winesburg, was there. He stayed in a corner and for the most part said nothing…Enoch wanted to talk too but he didn't know how. He was too excited to talk coherently. When he tried he sputtered and stammered and his voice sounded strange and squeaky to him. (200)

In autistic fashion, Enoch remains alone even in a crowd, tries to speak but cannot, and finds the social experience completely overwhelming. His solution is to lock the door and keep the artists away. Frustrated by his lack of social ease, he retreats into solitude. At night, he wanders the streets alone.

Enoch's remedy is to replace the people with fantasy characters that he invents and can manipulate. He retreats into a make-believe world filled with imaginary characters he controls: "He wanted most of all the people of his own mind, people with whom he could really talk, people he could harangue and scold by the hour, servants, you see, to his fancy. Among these people he was always self-confident and bold… They might talk…but always he talked last and best" (202). Enoch is described as being child-like when he retreats to this fantasy world. Like Temple Grandin, Donna Williams, Daniel Tammet, and Opal Whiteley, Enoch has invented "people" with whom he can socialize comfortably—people who are good listeners, who admire their host, and who bring out the best in their quirky friend. Enoch finds great happiness when he has the opportunity to withdraw from the real world and join them.

In one final attempt to re-join society, Enoch marries a girl he meets in an art class. The marriage seems satisfactory at first, and they have two children. But after a few years, the narrator tells us that "he began to feel choked and walled in by the life in the apartment, and to feel toward his wife and even toward his children as he had felt concerning the [real] friends who once came to visit him" (204). Because he feels ill-equipped to handle these smothering relationships, he divorces his wife and sends her and the children away (just as Sherwood had done). She decides he is "slightly insane." For a while after this, he re-joins the fantasy friends.

Eventually, another real New York woman tries to enter his life. She is big, bold, brassy, and sensuous—Enoch is drawn to her but is simultaneously terrified: "I was afraid… I was terribly afraid… She was so grown up, you see" (209). Although he is tempted, Enoch does not have the maturity he needs to enter into a sexual relationship with this woman. He is afraid of her, and afraid of his own inability to make things work. Like Sherwood he is drawn to women but anxious about relationships that require adult participation—he is still child-like in his emotional capabilities.

By the end of the story Enoch is an old man, and he returns to Winesburg, "alone and defeated" (208). One night he decides he wants to share his story with someone. He meets George on the sidewalk near Elmer's shabby store on Maumee St. They chat for a bit, and then Enoch invites George up to his sitting room. In a "queer way," Enoch tells George about the apartment in New York and the people. He tells George about the woman, and how he felt trapped by her. "Things went to smash," Enoch tells George. He says that with this woman, "I would be submerged, drowned out." Enoch becomes agitated by the memories and George takes his leave. Enoch mutters to himself, "I'm alone, all alone here… It was warm and friendly in my room [with the fantasy friends], but now I'm all alone" (212).

This short story resembles "Queer" in a few important ways. In both stories, the protagonist is a man with an autistic presentation. Neither Elmer nor Enoch is able to interact socially with the other characters in a satisfactory way. Neither man is able to communicate effectively. Both of them have strange obsessions. Their strange ways alienate people, and they become very lonely.

In both stories, the setting is a symbolic portrayal of the main character's oddness and difference from the others. Both characters live in dreary, dark, dirty, and isolated places.

Finally, the same themes are developed in both stories—the themes of difference, loneliness, isolation, and alienation. Although George tries to befriend both individuals, in the end each one of them remains alone. The friendships are destined to fail. The endings are not very hopeful.

"Hands"

There are several other stories in *Winesburg, Ohio* that present characters on the spectrum who are alienated from their community, but the story "Hands," about the strange character Wing Biddlebaum, is perhaps the most famous. Like Elmer and Enoch, Wing inhabits a setting that emphasizes his isolation:

> Upon the half decayed veranda of a small frame house that stood near the edge of a ravine near the town of Winesburg, Ohio, a fat little old man walked nervously up and down. Across a long field that has been seeded for clover but that had produced only a dense crop of yellow mustard weeds, he could see the public highway... [He] did not think of himself as in any way a part of the life of the town where he had lived for twenty years. (7)

Wing has lived enshrouded in a life of "long years of silence," unable to speak to neighbors, unable to make friends, unable to join the groups of people who pass his house on the highway. He seeks invisibility, but one thing that draws unwanted attention his way is the constant flapping of his hands: "The slender expressive fingers, forever active, forever striving to conceal themselves in his pockets or behind his back, came forth and became the piston rods of his machinery of expression" (9). He tries to hide his hand motions but can't, and this hand-flapping makes him into a bizarre and hideous character: "they made more grotesque an already grotesque and elusive individuality" (10). Hand-flapping, of course, is one visible trait of autism spectrum disorder.

In Winesburg, Wing is a self-styled outcast. The narrator informs us that in his youth he had been an outstanding teacher of boys in a small town in Pennsylvania. His poetic and sensitive nature gave him a great compassion for youngsters, and he had a gift for loving, encouraging, and inspiring the boys in his care. What happens next is unclear. The narrator tells us that Wing's caresses were platonic expressions of affection. The adult men of the town believe Wing to be a pedophile whose hands have touched the children inappropriately. Wing seems to think the hands have a life of their own and that they move without his willing them. At any rate, after a "half-wit" boy reveals something that might only be a fantasy, Wing is captured, beaten, humiliated, and run out of town. He narrowly escapes being lynched. Anderson's sympathy for Wing might be enhanced by the fact that as a boy Anderson, like Wing, had once been beaten and humiliated by a crowd of angry boys—both Anderson and Wing were "pelted with mud" (Anderson *Memoirs* 47).

Escaping Pennsylvania for Ohio, Wing goes to live with an elderly aunt who leaves her farm to him. For 20 years he huddles in the house, "striving to conceal his hands." The narrator stresses that Wing does not understand what had happened or why the men had beaten him. He is unable to decode their references to his hands as the perpetrators of sexual offenses; he merely grasps the literal meaning that his hands are bad. He does not have the "theory of mind" to understand why they are so furious with him. Even though 20 years have passed, Wing seems trapped by his situation. He doesn't have the wherewithal to start afresh or improve his life. He is prone to pacing nervously back and forth. He can never teach again, and is unable to do any kind of work besides picking crops.

Biddlebaum the silent seldom talks to anyone, but with George Willard he "talks excitedly" until his voice becomes "shrill and loud." His body "wriggles" and moves "convulsively." When he is especially excited, he pounds on tabletops or fence posts. George is curious about Wing Biddlebaum. He spends time with the old man occasionally, and offers a quiet, accepting friendship. Wing adores George, and offers him the same kind of advice he had offered his young students: "You must forget all you have learned," Wing tells him, "you must begin to dream. From this time on you must shut your ears to the roaring of the voices" (12). George wants to know more about the hands, but respects Wing's dignity enough to keep silent about them. George's friendship means everything to Wing, but Wing ends the conversation prematurely by nervously saying that he can't talk any more. Once home, he again paces nervously back and forth.

The final image of Wing is stunning in its strange beauty. In the evening, alone in his dark kitchen, Wing lights a lamp and prepares himself two slices of bread and honey. After eating them, he goes through something that seems to be an evening ritual for him:

> A few stray white bread crumbs lay on the cleanly washed floor by the table; putting the lamp upon a low stool he began to pick up the crumbs, carrying them to his mouth one by one with unbelievable rapidity. In the dense blotch of light beneath the table, the kneeling figure looked like a priest engaged in some service of his church. The nervous expressive fingers flashing in and out of the light might well have been mistaken for the fingers of the devotee going swiftly through decade after decade of his rosary. (17)

Anderson paints a haunting image here that is laden with symbolism. Wing undergoes a type of penance here, earning forgiveness for his sins. Through the repetitive motion of his "evil" hands, he transforms the floor from dirty to clean. It is a kind of prayerful meditation that he performs, and this ritual has the power to help Wing feel clean enough to find peace in the sleep that will follow. This ritual seems particularly autistic to me—the emphasis on the tiny parts that are moved from floor to mouth, the single-mindedness of purpose, the solitary nature of his occupation. Most people would have grabbed a broom and swept the crumbs out the back door, but by completing this ritual, Wing partakes of a religious cleansing and starts the process of healing. His time with George has been therapeutic after all, although it is doubtful their friendship can progress much further.

Wing resembles Elmer and Enoch in his odd presentation, his isolation from others, and his feelings of alienation. Like them, he is frustrated by his inability to improve his situation. Like them he is lonely, and in his loneliness reaches out to young George Willard. These three characters can be traced back to Sherwood's brother Earl, the "strange one" who "felt sad and felt unwanted" his entire life (Cox). Like Earl they all have speech problems, they have tics that drive people crazy, they can not find gainful employment, and they withdraw from the world. They are also like Earl in this regard: there is one person they feel they can trust enough to seek out. George, like Sherwood, is a compassionate fellow human. George, like Sherwood, seems to understand. He realizes that "the grotesques are the people whose humanity has been outraged; their need for love has been met with callousness, misunderstanding, or indifference" (Mishra 72). George is willing to listen calmly. He accepts them as they are. I am reminded here of the advice that a saloon keeper once gave young Sherwood regarding his father Irwin: "Do not think too badly of your father. He is what he is. He cannot be different. He is a good fellow. He's all right. Someday you will understand him better than you do now" (Anderson *Memoirs* 101). *Winesburg, Ohio* is the story of grotesques, but the story of grotesques who might find a friend in George Willard, even if they cannot find complete satisfaction in life.

Crossing Genres

Winesburg, Ohio is a hybrid between a novel and a collection of short stories. It has the features of a novel in that all events take place in one town (Winesburg) and one time period (1880s or 1890s). It feels like a novel if you follow the story of George Willard, the central character, and consider that he appears in or is named in 18 out of 24 stories. In this sense, one might take the collection for a *Bildungsroman,* in that George's growth and development is chronicled throughout the book. The stories may be viewed as chapters, working together to create a loosely developed narrative about a young man who lives in a small town, and eventually leaves it.

Yet the book also has features of a collection of short stories. Each of the 24 stories is self-contained and can stand alone as an individual unit. Each story focuses on a different resident of Winesburg, and has a different point of view. Even though George is alluded to in many of the stories, some stories are clearly about other characters. In a story such as "Adventure," for example, we are only told that Alice was a grown up woman when George was a child, and that her boyfriend, Ned Currie, works at the same newspaper where George works. Other than that, it is clearly Alice's story, and it is told from her point of view. Reading the stories feels more like watching a slide show than a movie: they are random, static glimpses of a community, and do not form a coherent, sustained narrative from beginning to end.

Anderson's breakthrough in creating this hybrid genre is incredibly important to American literature. In daring to publish a book that seemed to be almost a misfit, he boldly established a new genre that many American writers would use for generations to follow. In creating the "short story cycle," Anderson knew he had taken a quantum leap forward in his writing and had made a new path in American literature.

What role did autism play in the development of this new genre? If we consider what research tells us about the mind of a person on the spectrum, we know that there can be a tendency to struggle with executive function, and that the ability to sustain a "master narrative" can be a challenge. Matthew Belmonte's research on autistic brains led him to conclude that

> Autism's characteristic pattern of impairment in cognitive tasks that demand contextual processing and superiority at tasks that demand piecemeal processing of individual features has been described as "weak central coherence" [Frith 1989; Happé 1996], that is, an abnormally weak tendency to bind local details into global percepts. (3)

In other words, we might expect that a writer with autism would have an easier time writing poetry or short stories or essays, since these are more likely to use "piecemeal processing," and a harder time writing novels or other lengthy books that demand "contextual processing." Anderson felt this in writing the novels that preceded *Winesburg*—they were harder to write and not as successful as works of art. One reviewer said his novels lacked plot: "never was a man more harassed for something for his characters to do" (Smith 93). But in linking separate tales together in pastiche fashion rather than a linear storyline, he was satisfying his own impulse to focus on smaller, separate tales rather than one structured narrative. It worked.

One critic noted that "the short story [genre] allowed him to harmonize form with content: his concerns with the fragmentary nature of modern life is mirrored in the fragmentary glimpses he gives us of individuals in his short tales" (Dunne 109). I would also argue that by using a "loosely connected" short story format, Anderson was symbolically demonstrating how the autistic citizens of Winesburg stay separated from each other and from the community, each in his own silo, even though they all live together in the same geographical town. Only George Willard is able to touch so many other characters. Anderson once said that *Winesburg* was the book that told the truth of his childhood. In talking about his writing process, he added that "I have no desire to put down, in chronological order, the incidental acts of [my] life but there is a loose structure, a rambling sort of house, of many rooms, occupied by many people, of which I would like to tell" (*Memoirs* 28). These "rambling rooms" are the individual stories of people like Elmer and Enoch and Wing and George.

Structure: Multiple Points of View

Central to the structure of *Winesburg, Ohio* is the use of multiple points of view. Anderson uses a third person voice throughout the book, but each story focuses on the perspective of one citizen of Winesburg. Anderson the writer seizes the opportunity to "try on" all sorts of identities that Anderson the man might have been curious about: a lonely young woman, a stubborn old man, a fat doctor, a tired mother, a journalist, a sinful preacher, a teacher. Secrets of one character are revealed to the reader but not the other characters, such as the painful revelation after Elizabeth Willard's paralyzing stroke that she has hidden her son's inheritance behind the plaster of a wall, never to be found (Earl also hid money in the wall of his New York apartment).

By going into the different minds of various characters, Anderson was making the same discoveries with pen and paper that artists over in Paris were making with paint and canvas: they shattered reality into pieces or fragments that could be viewed from different perspectives, adding power and richness to Western art. Anderson's multi-faceted writing, like the paintings of Georges Braque, Picasso, and Juan Gris, contributed to the school of cubism that was setting fire to the art world. In *Winesburg*, just as in the paintings, the fragmented shards touch each other, overlap, twist around, and leave gaps. The character of Emma Willard, for example, appears worn-down yet sympathetic to her son George, but full of sensuous yearning to her friend Dr. Reefy. We never do find out what her husband thinks of her. In presenting these various angles, Anderson was making a breakthrough in literature that paved the way for modern and post-modern authors to follow. And even though the reviews of the book were not positive, Anderson still believed in himself and his writing abilities: he realized he was making an important contribution to literature. His innovation might not have been possible had he been a neurotypical writer who "followed the rules" because he worried too much about what others thought.

Anderson had struggled with the single-perspective novels that he had written previous to *Winesburg*, but the short story cycle with its different voices came to him easily. As a boy, Anderson watched his father change his own identity according to the person he was speaking to—his father could become Irish, Scotch, German, Swede, or any other nationality at the drop of a hat (*Memoirs* 79). Sherwood himself was personally familiar with the problem of shifting identity:

> [H]e sought an identity through the trying on of personalities... he was essentially a showman of the self and little more... everyone, he was convinced, was a mixture of selves, was one

> or more persons to the world while inwardly living constantly shifting "lives." (Rideout V1 310)

The fluidity of the self is a trait shared by many people on the spectrum: all of the autobiographers studied in this book, as well as many of the literary authors, had a fluid, plastic sense of who they were. An AS student of mine who shuffles about ten different identities calls it "changing his social armor." This shuffling can be beneficial for some kinds of creative writing, such as writing short stories, poetry, or drama. Michael Fitzgerald reminds us that:

> Such writers [with Asperger's] have huge problems [with] "self-construction." Paradoxically, these massive struggles can help them in their creative literary works. They have to construct deliberately what comes automatically for neurotypicals (non-autistic people). A great deal of literary writing is about "different selves," and people who have a problem with their sense of self are often the best at writing about it. This can lead to literary success. (*Genesis* 28)

Sherwood's older brother Karl pointed out that he thought there was a bit of Earl in every character in *Winesburg*—but it is just as true that there is a bit of Sherwood in every character as well.

Writing Style: Slippery Language

In the prologue story, "Book of the Grotesques," Anderson struggles to describe what is "in the heart" of the old writer who lies in his bed, thinking:

> He was like a pregnant woman, only that the thing inside him was not a baby but a youth. No, it wasn't a youth, it was a woman, young, and wearing a coat of mail like a knight. It is absurd, you see, to try to tell what was inside the old writer

> as he lay on his high bed and listened to the fluttering of his heart. (2)

Instead of telling us what is inside the writer, Anderson tosses out a few possibilities but ultimately leaves the reader hanging—why can't he settle on one? And why would it be "absurd" for him to try to explain to us what he is thinking? It seems that the narrator knows how unlikely it is that language can ever represent reality.

Anderson employs a similar type of strategy for describing Joe Welling, the talkative hero of "A Man of Ideas." Anderson writes: "He was like a tiny little volcano that lies silent for days and then suddenly spouts fire. No, he wasn't like that—he was like a man who is subject to fits, one who walks among his fellow men inspiring fear because a fit may come upon him suddenly and blow him away…" (110). Why does the narrator compare Joe to a volcano if that metaphor isn't right?

In another story, "Hands," Anderson describes the inspired teaching of Wing Biddlebaum, then immediately undercuts his own description: "In their feeling for the boys under their charge, such men [Wing] are not unlike the finer sort of women in their love of men. And yet that is but crudely stated. It needs the poet there." The reader is left wondering why Anderson leaves it to another writer to complete a description he has started. Is language an inadequate tool for translating a 3-D world onto a 2-D page? Could written language be an inadequate tool for presenting an autistic sensibility to a neurotypical audience?

When *Winesburg* was published, Anderson's circular, indirect writing was praised by some critics and condemned by others. French critic Jean Catel was bewildered by Anderson's use of language, calling it "strange": "neither order nor style. A confusion that envelops you, drowns you, pushes you, leaving you breathless. Events don't follow with that logic novelists know how to introduce into the complexity of life. They advance only after brusque and multiple backtrackings. One step forward leads to ten steps backward" (Schriber 144). Other critics and readers echoed this frustration with Anderson's writing style—it is at once direct, in how he honestly addresses the reader; and indirect, in that he does not fulfill the reader's expectation.

In trying to understand *why* Anderson wrote as he did, Catel added: "one suspects in Anderson the desire to avoid the usual processes of writing in order to respect the astonishing richness of the flow of living language" (Schriber 143). Here he compliments Anderson for leaving behind the artificial formalism of Victorian prose, and for avoiding the "usual processes" of pretending that language can capture reality.

Of course there are many possible reasons why Anderson used this unique writing style in *Winesburg* and other texts. The most likely, in my opinion, is that he was caught up in the *avant-garde* zeitgeist of his time period, and wanted, like so many others, to "make it new." Michael Fitzgerald identifies "autistic imagination" and "novelty seeking" as characteristics common to people with AS (*Genesis* 105). He believes that AS individuals are "child-like" and "non-conformist" in their outlook. These traits might help us to understand why Anderson broke out of traditional structures *and* styles when writing his short story cycle.

It might be fruitful here to compare Anderson to two of his contemporaries who also showed traits of Asperger's Syndrome (see Michael Fitzgerald's *Genesis*). Béla Bartók (1881–1945) was an Austro-Hungarian composer who experimented with music the way Anderson experimented with language. Bartók was "ahead of his contemporaries. His genius rested in his unique approach to composition; he experimented with 'bitonality, dissonant counterpoint, chords in intervals other than thirds' before Stravinsky and Schoenberg did" (181). One can almost imagine the first listeners who heard this kind of music, covering their ears and asking themselves, "Is this *really* how it's supposed to sound?" Bartók's messing around with the normal, accepted tonalities in symphonic music is similar to what Anderson was doing with indirect descriptive language in his stories. Vincent Van Gogh (1853–1890), the Dutch painter who used swirling, twirling strokes of bright color to express his views of the world, also refused to follow the forms of conventional painting, leaving the viewer to wonder "is it a star, or a candle, or a reflection?" when viewing a painting such as Starry Night over the Rhone (1888). His use of color was as free-form as was Anderson's use of language. An in-depth comparison of these three geniuses would no doubt reveal interesting similarities in how each handles genre, perspective, and meaning.

Hans Asperger defined "autistic intelligence" as "a sort of intelligence hardly touched by tradition and culture—unconventional, unorthodox, strangely pure and original, akin to the intelligence of true creativity" (Fitzgerald *Autism* 5). Sherwood Anderson possessed such intelligence, and with this advantage he helped to usher in an entirely new way of writing short stories. He gave the world stories of middle-class and working-class people; stories of people down on their luck and down on themselves; stories of the brilliant, the stupid, and the half-witted. He gave us a new genre, the "short story cycle" that gives us the pleasure of the short tale with the satisfaction of the novel. He traded universal Truth for "truth" told in multiple perspectives. He showed us how indirect language can resonate more realistically than the direct. His beloved friend Gertrude Stein, who knew him well and knew his stories even better, had this to say about his autobiography, but the words describe *Winesburg* as well: "The story-teller's story is not a story of events or experiences it is a story of existence, and the fact that the story teller exists makes a story and keeps on making a story. The story-teller's story will live because the story-teller is alive. As he is alive and as his gift is the complete expression of that life it will continue to live" (Anderson *Storyteller* xix). Sherwood Anderson's gift was to create a work of literature that challenges the reader's expectations. But his gift was also to tell stories about people the neurotypical world needs to notice and pay attention to, people like his brother Earl. Sherwood had a tender place in his heart for his struggling little brother, and seemed to understand his pain as no one else could, perhaps because some of those struggles were his as well.

Works Cited

Anderson, Karl. *Reminiscences of Sherwood.* As told to Anne Poor. November 14, 1964. Kindly given to the author by Dorothy Cox and the Clyde, Ohio Public Library.

Anderson, Sherwood. *Sherwood Anderson's Memoirs.* Ed. Ray Lewis White. Chapel Hill: University of North Carolina Press, 1969.

---. *A Storyteller's Story.* Ed. Ray Lewis White. Cleveland: Case Western Reserve University, 1968.

---. *Winesburg, Ohio.* New York: Random House, The Modern Library Edition, 1947. All quotations from *Winesburg* are from this edition.

Belmonte, Matthew K. "Human, but More So: What the Autistic Brain Tells Us about the Process of Narrative." Paper presented to Autism and Representation Conference, Case Western Reserve University, Cleveland, Ohio, October 28–30 2005. http://www.cwru.edu. Used by permission.

Cox, Dorothy. Personal Interview. June 27, 2008. Clyde, Ohio.

Dunne, Robert. *A New Book of the Grotesques.* Kent, Ohio: Kent State University, 2005.

Fitzgerald, Michael. *Autism and Creativity: Is there a Link between Autism in Men and Exceptional Ability?* New York: Brunner-Routledge, 2004.

---. *The Genesis of Artistic Creativity: Asperger's Syndrome and the Arts.* London: Jessica Kingsley Publishers, 2005.

Mishra, Ajit Kumar. *Loneliness in Modern American Fiction.* Delhi: Authors Guild Publications, 1984.

Rideout, Walter B. *Sherwood Anderson: A Writer in America.* Vol 1 and 2. Madison: University of Wisconsin Press, 2006 and 2007.

Schriber, Marysue. "Sherwood Anderson in France: 1919–1939." *Twentieth Century Literature* 23.1. February 1977: 140–153.

Smith, Rachel. "Sherwood Anderson: Some Entirely Arbitrary Reactions." In David D. Anderson, *Critical Essays on Sherwood Anderson.* Boston: G. K. Hall and Company, 1981. 92–95.

CHAPTER NINE

Opal Whiteley

Opal Whiteley, Child Author

It's no surprise that scholars as well as readers remain interested in the story of Opal Whiteley (1897–1992). Her diary of childhood, *The Story of Opal* (1920), was an instant best seller, both in America and in England, and everyone (even Theodore Roosevelt, the President of France, and the Queen of Belgium) was reading it. The diary covers approximately one year in the life of a small girl who lives deep in the wild Oregon forest. The diary records incidents from her daily life such as doing chores at home for her mother and walking to a country school each day. More importantly, it describes the imaginative play of young Opal as she spends her free time roaming the Oregon forests, climbing trees and taming wild animals. She comes across as a girl with a rich imaginative life and a poetic, creative way of using language. She also comes across as an odd and lonely child who never could figure out who she was or who she belonged with. The diary gives us a rare, valuable glimpse into the mind of a little girl who presented signs of Asperger's Syndrome (AS).

Sadly, as quickly as the unusual diary rose to fame, it sank to notoriety—in part because the reading public decided it could not make sense of its peculiar author. Opal's place on the autism spectrum contributed to her brilliance as a writer, but also, unfortunately, prevented her from being accepted and respected as an author.

Opal Whiteley and Asperger's Syndrome

Opal was born in 1897 in rural Washington to a pioneer woman, Lizzie Whiteley, and her logger husband Ed. A few years after Opal's birth, the family moved to Oregon, where her father found work in the logging camps of the Coast Range Mountains and her mother tried to keep a decent home out in the wilds. Lizzie, Opal's mother, was eccentric: when company would call, she would run into the woods to hide. She could sometimes be found hiding up in trees. She was fond of saying that Opal was not her real daughter, and spanked her excessively. People thought she was strange. Not much is known about Opal's father or siblings.

Opal was an extremely intelligent girl. In the one-room country school she attended, she finished first and second grade in one year. She read every book she could find, and her teacher had boxes of books sent over from the state library in Salem so Opal could study independently. She loved history and poetry. She devoured sentimental novels, but sometimes couldn't remember if the events happened to a character or to her. She loved to write and was often seen writing in her diary. Her favorite subject in school was natural science—she could name all of the local plants and animals both with common names and Latin names. "When it came to natural history, her photographic memory and her enthusiasm kicked in, and she overwhelmed everyone, including the teacher. Sometimes her teacher simply turned the class over to her" (Beck 24).

At age 17 she visited the University of Oregon to show the science faculty a rare mineral specimen she had found—they were so impressed with her intelligence and knowledge of natural science that they offered her scholarships and early admission on the spot. They declared they had never seen such a young scholar who knew so much about the natural environment. One professor noted, "She knows more about geology than do many students that have graduated from my department. She may become one of the greatest minds Oregon has ever produced. She will be an investment for the university" (Beck 24). While in college she combined two interests—writing and science—by writing a natural history book for children, called *The Fairyland around Us.* When she could not find a publisher for the book, she published it herself, which proved to be an overwhelming task.

Opal showed signs of Asperger's Syndrome from a young age. She suffered from sensory issues and seemed to be oblivious to cold, to hunger, and to pain. She often either forgot to eat or else shared her food with wild animals. As a teenager, she lost both her hearing and her speech for three months after she suffered a nervous breakdown. She was clumsy and was always dropping things. Her vision was so acute she could see individual leaves, caterpillars, and tiny rodents at great distances. Her hearing was so sharp she could hear leaves rustling, mice chattering, and all kinds of tiny sounds that most people would not notice. She also had synesthesia: her vision and hearing were sometimes entwined, which added unusual beauty to her writing.

She exhibited other stereotyped behaviors common to those with AS. She would line up things like potatoes into long rows. She had many rituals such as counting objects and actions. She was obsessive about giving every animal she encountered a very complicated name (she named a wood mouse Thomas Chatterton Jupiter Zeus). The calendar was important to her: she kept track of the "borning days" and "going away days" of medieval royalty and famous people. She engaged in bizarre rituals to commemorate those days such as lining up potatoes in rows, tying leaves to tree limbs, and chanting Latin phrases in the pig pen. By all accounts she was a quirky little girl.

Throughout her life, Opal struggled with social skills. She was not able to sustain a back and forth conversation with others, but instead would lecture people she met about her favorite topics (science, nature, royal families). As a child she did not play with other children, but she did enjoy visiting some of the adults who lived in the vicinity. Children with Asperger's Syndrome often relate better to adults than to other children. The other teenaged girls were mean to her and taunted her, "even to her face" (Beck 16). In college, at a tea party she hosted, her guests commented that there was no polite small talk because Opal was feverishly lecturing everybody about nature in a high-pitched voice (Fortt). At a dinner gathering, "Opal contributed nothing to the conversation. She answered in monotone syllables, her eyes on her plate" (Hoff 14).

When she was 20 the Atlantic Monthly Press published her diary about her childhood, *The Story of Opal*, and she rode a wave of fame for some time. She grew excited by the possibility of earning a living by her writing. But then the public started to ask her questions about herself that, as a woman with autism, she was not equipped to answer: Who was she? What was her background? What was she like? Where did her writing talent come from? Like many people on the spectrum, Opal suffered from "identity diffusion" and her sense of self was never fixed. Because of this, she answered the questions in many conflicting ways. For publicity, she had herself photographed in a variety of costumes and poses, and "tried on" several ethnic identities. She claimed two different "fathers" and several different "mothers." Like Hans Christian Andersen, she fantasized that she was descended from royalty. Like Lewis Carroll, she used more than one name. People kept demanding that Opal reveal her "true self" to the world, and as a person who had autism this was something she could not do. The tide of popularity then turned against her and she crashed. She wrote very little after this, and was forced to live with a series of friends and acquaintances since she was unable to support herself any other way.

As an older woman, Opal lived in London, where her cognitive abilities seemed to disintegrate. She kept to a tiny apartment, safe in a fortress of books, living off money that people gave her. During World War II, she was seen picking books out of piles of bombed out rubbish. She had been spending her money on books, rather than food, and she was starving. When Opal was 50, the London authorities finally rescued her from this horrible situation and took her to a mental institution in the country, where she could be fed and properly looked after. When she was committed to Napsbury Hospital in England, the officials boxed up 800 crates of books and put them into storage. She received few visitors, and remained there until her death in 1992.

Writing Process

The Story of Opal reads like a diary written by a child, but evidence suggests that she wrote part of it as a child, and part of it as a young woman looking back at her childhood. We don't know for sure how Opal wrote her diary, but if we take her word for it, she printed the diary each day on sheets of paper, and then stored the diary pages in a box. At some point her sister tore the pages into little bits, then the bits were hidden in another box. Years later they were reconstructed, edited, and typed for publication. This "cut and paste" method for producing a manuscript is similar to the way Lewis Carroll cut up his manuscript of *Sylvie and Bruno* and then re-constructed it before its publication. It is similar to the way Hans Christian Andersen cut up letters and articles to paste into his autobiography. There seems to be an impulse to create—and to destroy—occurring simultaneously. The manuscript, like the author's identity, is presented in taped-together fragments.

Opal's writing process resembles that of other AS writers in another important way: the content of her writing was heavily influenced by what she read. While she was a student at the University of Oregon, she wrote in a notebook a list of "books read at age 15." It is a list of sentimental novels written for teenaged girls. I gathered up that collection of books and read them all, and it became clear to me where many of Opal's ideas came from. They came from these novels.

Opal's writing process was similar to Hans Christian Andersen's when he was a young writer just starting out: cut a little of this and a little of that, paste it all together, and call it your own. I believe her photographic memory comes into play here: she read a large number of books, remembered them all, and when it came time for *her* to write, the jumbled combination of memories couldn't help but stream out from her pen. In *The Anxiety of Influence*, Harold Bloom observes that everything a person writes is actually a revision of something he has read. In the case of an autistic writer, this connection between the read and the written is more heavily pronounced. But the peculiar thing about Opal's text is that she didn't try to disguise what she was doing. She either thought the reader wouldn't notice she was borrowing ideas, or else she thought they wouldn't care. Or, she may not have been aware that she was "rewriting" the sentimental novels of her youth. This is where an autistic lack of "theory of mind" comes into play—Opal did not consider the reader's reaction to a work that contained recycled material.

A quick look at some of these texts reveals the connection between what Opal read and what she wrote. Indeed, both her text *and* her own evolving self-identity emerged as a collage of the sentimental novels she read as a teenaged girl:

1. Opal's favorite book was apparently *Rebecca of Sunnybrook Farm* (Kate Douglas Wiggin, 1903), since she not only read it but also wrote a reminder to herself to "study" the book. Rebecca is a poor girl who goes to live with a rich family. At school one day, Rebecca's teacher punishes her for something that isn't her fault, and makes her stand in the corner. This scene is repeated in Opal's diary. On another occasion, Rebecca is corrected for saying that hollyhocks are "glad." Many of the flowers in Opal's book are "glad." Rebecca is a creative soul who writes notes on leaves and casts them to the wind, a gesture that is repeated exactly in Opal's diary.

2. In *Freckles* (Gene Stratton Porter, 1904), a young orphan boy ends up living with a lumberjack foster family deep in the woods. Freckles loves the wild nature around him, and creates a "Cathedral" space in the clearing where he plants special flowers. He stores special books in a box he hides in the woods. The cathedral, the plants, and the secret box appear in Opal's diary as though she had thought of them herself. Freckles treasures and preserves the

footprint of a friend as it dries in the mud. Young Opal treasures the dried footprint of the family's cow, and puts it into a drawer for safe-keeping. Freckles refers to a bumpy dirt road as "the corduroy," and Opal also refers to "the corduroy road."

3. Elnora, *The Girl of the Limberlost* (Gene Stratton Porter, 1909), lives on the edge of a big forest. Her mother is cruel to her, always criticizing her and always piling on more chores. Elnora escapes from her mother and the mean kids at school by finding refuge in the beautiful forest, where she collects nature specimens. Like Opal, Elnora shares her meager lunch with the less fortunate. She, too, keeps her treasures in a "secret box" in the woods. Elnora is desperate to have a white fancy dress; Opal's friend Lola also yearns for a white fancy dress. There are so many similarities between this novel and Opal's diary that it seems Opal has become a Gene Stratton Porter character herself.

4. Opal's interest in fairies, which we find both in the diary and in *The Fairyland around Us*, derives from Arabella Buckley's *The Fairyland of Science* (1905), a book that teaches children about science through the metaphor of fairies. In Buckley's book, fairies make things happen. In Opal's diary, fairies carry messages and bring her crayons. In Buckley's book we read of "the journey of a raindrop" as it morphs from cloud to water to ice. In her diary, young Opal declares, "When I grow up, I am going to write a book about a raindrop's journey." Opal talks of hearing "voices" in nature; Buckley writes of hearing "voices of nature that speak to us from time to time."

This process suggests that Opal was not able to forge an original text for herself, but instead had to follow the path of other writers with autistic echolalia. She "mimicked" what she'd read and put it into print, just as some kids who have autism "mimic" what they hear and put it into speech. Some have been known to watch a television program once, and thereafter to recite the entire show from memory. Opal was able to read a book once and then "re-write" the details from the book into her own story. This could only have happened *after* she read the other books at age 15.

Unique, Original Language and Style

While it is true that the content of Opal's diary was derivative, her language and literary style is uniquely her own—it is quirky and poetic and fun. No other author working in English has a writing style similar to Opal's.

The opening sentences introduce us to not only the narrator, but also to her way of using language:

> TO-DAY the folks are gone away from the house we do live in. They are gone a little way away, to the ranch-house where the grandpa does live. I sit on our steps and I do print. I like it—this house we do live in being at the edge of the near woods. So many little people do live in the near woods. I do have conversations with them. I found the near woods first day I did go explores. That was the next day after we were come here. (Hoff)

Instead of saying "house" she says "the house we do live in." And she describes the house "where grandpa does live." She "did go" explores, and so on. Her use of indicative "do" here and throughout the text, a kind of verbal tic, is an odd English usage. It resembles the overly formal speech that a child with Asperger's Syndrome might use. In other places, she uses a grammatical style that sounds somewhat "Frenchified": "I have hunger," "the mamma did have needs of me," and so on.

Not only does her syntax somewhat resemble French, but Opal also uses many French words and sayings in her diary. She uses the French names for animals: *cochon, mulot, daine, canard, dindon, poisson, poulain,* and *merle*. She knows the names of French rivers, and chants them to her baby sister: *Adour, Avre, Ain, Aube, Arroux*, and *Allier*. She knows the French names of many flowers she collects. This merging of English with French occurs in several places and creates a highly idiosyncratic, fragmented linguistic style.

Opal's syntax is further fragmented by her occasional use of King James English, which she undoubtedly picked up from reading her Bible for Sunday school. In one scene she reassures a pet piglet that "the hairs of thy baby head, they are numbered" (222). In another, she is playing in the pigpen and she declares, "I will lift up mine eyes unto the hills" (263). The language of Opal's diary shows traces of both English Protestant and French Catholic influences.

Opal liked to pretend that she was a French princess who was adopted by a poor American family. We might view Opal's peculiar syntax as her attempt to sound like a French girl who has been transplanted to the backwoods of Oregon. Or, we might just view her idiosyncratic syntax as her own unique creation. Daniel Tammet was fascinated by words and language to the extent that he wanted to create a language of his own:

> For several years as a child I tinkered with the idea of creating my own language, as a way of relieving the loneliness I often felt and to draw on the delight I experienced in words… I continued to dream that one day I would speak a language that was my own, that I would not be teased or reprimanded for using, and that would express something of *what it felt to be me*." (Tammet 170, emphasis added)

Opal wraps herself in a language of her own making as a way to soften the blows of the world. The language expresses *what it felt to be her.*

For Opal, as for Lewis Carroll and James Joyce, words were like toys—she could get them out and "play" with them whenever she was feeling lonely or bored. She loved to learn new words, like "screw tin ize," and she liked to make up new words, like "chapine" (hooded). Opal was so fascinated by language that she spent hours poring over books, mesmerized by what she often called "the spell of the words."

Opal's use of descriptive language is further enriched by her synesthesia. She describes visions as having sounds, and sounds as having color. Some examples from the diary: Grandpa's temper has bumps all over it (104); the cow's mooings are very musical and there is poetry in her tracks (135); when Opal listens to a cocoon, she "hears the sound of its feels" (143); she understands that a blind girl has "seeings by feels" (143); shadows have "such velvety fingers" (145); and lichens speak in "gray tones" (194). When a mother sings a lullaby to her baby, Opal sees the musical notes dancing above the baby's cradle (214). Researchers at the California Center for Brain Studies have linked synesthesia, which is neurologically based, with linguistic creativity—the condition is seven times more prevalent in creative people than in the general public (Tammet 163).

There is a peculiar montage quality to Opal's prose style that is almost Joycean. At times she speaks as a girl might write to her diary: "Some days are long. Some days are short. The days that I have to stay in the house are the most long days of all." Sometimes she uses language the way a very young child might, complete with best-guess spelling: invest tag ashuns, at ten chuns, new sance. Sometimes she gives geology lectures. Sometimes she waxes philosophical: "I have thinks pigs do have likes for clean places to live in—it brings more inspiration to their souls" (250). Other times, her prose is pure poetry:

> Earth-voices are glad voices, and earth-songs come up from the ground through the plants; and in their flowering, and in the days before these days are come, they do tell the earth-songs to the wind. And the wind in her goings does whisper them to folks to print for other folks, so other folks do have knowing of earth's songs. (121)

Opal explored language. She "tried on" different speech patterns. With the help of her editor, Ellery Sedgwick, these voices were spliced together into the format of a little girl's story. Opal needed the help of an editor like Sedgwick to help her smooth out her unusual writing style for a reading public, just as Temple Grandin and other writers on the spectrum have needed assistance with editing when they wish to appeal to a larger, neurotypical audience.

Opal's other book, *The Fairyland Around Us*, which was written to teach children about science, also comes across as a peculiar hodgepodge of linguistic style. In this book Opal employs various points of view (I, we, they, you), different authorial stances (Opal as child, Opal as teacher, Opal as expert), several genres (a fairy tale, a science book, a memoir, and a manual), a wide variety of voices, and a very odd jumble of illustrations that she *literally* cut out of other people's books to paste into her own manuscripts. One critic remarked:

> Technically it is a disaster, and the prose is uneven and often arch with many sentences starting with "'Tis" and "'Twas." Mind-numbing too are the long lists of species and their classifications. It also has the appearance of having been put together rather hastily... Despite the scattered nature of the book, there are some charming bits of imagery. (Beck 49)

Since she published this book by herself, and had *no* editorial help in pulling it all together, all of the "rough edges" are revealed. But I disagree that the "scattered nature" of the book was due to a "hasty" production process. I think that Opal, as a writer with autism, was simply unequipped to provide the organizational framework that the material required of her.

A Fragmented Narrative Strategy

The narrator of this diary presents a fragmented self. There are two girls here: the American Opal and her French alter-ego, Françoise. The book is given the title *The Story of Opal*, and the name Opal Whiteley appears on the cover. But she never refers to herself by that name in the diary, and neither do the other human characters. Natural beings, such as trees, grass, or breezes, refer to her by another name—*Petite Françoise.* As she walks through the woods, the trees call out to her: "*Come, petite Françoise.*" Later on, she pets a fuzzy pussy willow, and it calls to her, "*Bonjour, petite Françoise*!"

And again, on a windy day she is cheered by the voices of the grasses, who inform her of summer's approach: "*Petite Françoise—l'été approche, l'été approche*" (252). The diary never directly says who Françoise is, or why an American narrator refers to herself by this French name. The other human characters aren't helpful here, for they do not address her by either name—they only use generic terms for her such as "child" or "little one." It seems that Opal has, at this point, divided herself into two persons: the Oregon girl of the woods, and a little French maiden.

Why does she do this? It's possible that creating the "Françoise" identity was just a game to her, a game of pretend or make-believe. But it's also possible she took on the second identity as a means of distancing herself from her family. Her mother repeatedly said, out of frustration, that Opal was "not her real daughter." Opal probably heard this and, in autistic fashion, understood it literally—if she wasn't Lizzie's daughter, well, then she had to be somebody else. In the diary, Lizzie is portrayed as an abusive mother who repeatedly spanks Opal and puts her under the bed for punishment. It may have been comforting to the little girl to think she was secretly somebody else's child.

It is very illuminating here to compare Opal not to mainstream neurotypical writers, but to other writers on the spectrum. I am reminded here of one author's careful use of *Lewis Carroll* when he referred to himself as a writer, and *Charles Dodgson* when he referred to himself as a mathematician. If an Oxford colleague slipped and referred to him as "Carroll," he did not respond. Two names represented two distinctly separate parts of his identity.

I am also reminded of Donna Williams, who wrote a four-part autobiography that has many structural, stylistic, and thematic similarities to Opal Whiteley's diary of childhood. In the first installment, *Nobody Nowhere,* Williams explains that as a child with autism growing up in an abusive household, she spliced her identity into three selves as a matter of self-defense. There was the flesh and blood Donna who was always confused and who lived in a world of her own. In her autobiography, Donna explains how she always "became Willie" when she needed to be tough and stand up for herself. Donna "became Carol" (smiling, laughing, accommodating) when she wanted to please other people. Like Opal, Williams managed a stressful family life by fracturing her identity.

As part of this alternative identity, Opal writes about two sets of parents. She lives with "the mamma" and "the papa," ordinary Oregonians who do not understand or appreciate her. But when she is feeling sad or neglected, her mind turns to her "Angel Mother" and "Angel Father," her *real* parents. In this scenario, her *real* father is Prince Henri of France, last survivor of the Royal House of Bourbon. Her mother's identity is less certain, but she is certainly royal, and Opal pretends she died in a tragic accident, which explains why she cannot raise Opal herself.

When Opal "becomes Françoise," she becomes a person whose difference makes her special. As Françoise, she is French, she is royalty, and she is much loved by her *real* family. Through Françoise, Opal dreams of achieving grandness in her life, just like Andersen's little mermaid, ugly duckling, and match girl. Françoise isn't just the odd girl who annoys the teacher and alienates the other children at school. She's a princess who deserves respect. But the consequence of sustaining this fantasy is the fragmentation of Opal's being and of her narrative.

Writing to Repair: Toward a Cohesive Self

Here I turn to the research of Matthew Belmonte, who argues that the act of "creating narrative" springs from the human impulse to create cohesive meaning in the face of the chaotic sensory world we live in. All people act upon this impulse, but, according to Belmonte, the task is somewhat different for people who have autism. He attributes the ability to create narrative to the "executive function" of the brain, which creates over-arcing meaning out of fragments. If the executive function is impaired, it follows that the ability to create narrative will be impacted in some way. He speaks of the autistic mind as having "impairment in cognitive tasks that demand contextual processing," i.e. narrative connectivity, yet at the same time the autistic mind shows "superiority at tasks that demand piecemeal processing of individual features," i.e. brilliance in language usage in discreet settings. In other words, Opal's use of language was skillful—her ability to sustain the expected "traditional narrative" was not.

Belmonte further asserts that, in the face of narrative disruption, an autistic mind creates "fallback cognitive strategies" in order to form associations and, essentially, to create a new kind of narrative structure, or a new way of "making sense" out of the world (11). We saw this in Sherwood Anderson's invention of a new hybrid genre. We saw this in Emily Dickinson's original approach to writing poems. The desire to create narrative cohesion is strong in Opal's writings, but she must create it in different ways.

For example, autistic children usually struggle with social interactions. The fallback strategy is to "stand at the edge of a group and mimic its activities without engaging in its social give and take" (11). Opal cannot write the narrative of "Opal and her friends" or "Opal and her family," so she creates parallel structures to compensate. Instead of talking about how she and her family attend church together on Sunday mornings, for instance, she talks about how she, all alone, leads church services for the animals in the woods. Opal cannot write the narrative of "Opal at her girlfriend's birthday party," so she mimics such an occasion by celebrating, all alone, the birthdays of dead kings and queens. In this way the diary makes up for missing "girl diary narratives" by creating "alternative narratives" to take their places.

Children with autism also struggle with pragmatic speech and communication. For them, the fallback strategy is that the child "replaces [pragmatic speech] with rote phrases and with self-directed discourses on topics that s(he) knows well" (Belmonte 11). One might easily imagine that most "little girl diaries" would contain summaries of conversations that had occurred between the author and her friends or family. But in Opal's diary, there is no dialogue and there are no summaries of conversations. When her teacher unfairly sends her home from school early, one might think Opal would complain about it to somebody. Instead, she writes about going into the woods to dig up 45 plants. She carries them to her favorite place in the woods and explains to her pig that she plants these in honor of Girolamo Savonarola (a 15th century Catholic reformer) because that day it is his birthday and he lived to be 45. In another passage, when Opal's beloved dog is missing, a neighbor man asks Opal where she's looked for it, and she answers him with something like a map of France: "And he did ask where all I was going on searches. I did tell him to *Orne* and *Yonne* and *Rille*, and to *Camargue* and *Picardie* and *Auvergne*, and to the *Forêt de Montmorency*. And when I did so tell him, he did laugh." In this way Opal supplants normal conversation with lectures on her special interest topics. When a phrase catches her attention, such as "china mending glue guaranteed to stick," she repeats it over and over. Rote phrases replace normal conversation.

Sustained narrative is also made more difficult by "unscripted phenomenon" (Belmonte 11). The world is a very chaotic and unpredictable place, and a person with autism has neurological impairments that can make unexpected change very difficult to cope with. Parents of children with autism will tell you that most meltdowns happen when unexpected things occur. One way to ward off the unpredictable is to engage in ritual. Adding a good dose of ritual makes narratives predictable and thereby cohesive. Opal's diary is laced with ritual. She must give every animal she sees a name, and the name must be august (William Shakespeare the horse, Elizabeth Barrett Browning the cow, Aphrodite the pig, and so on). Opal must pay strict attention to the calendar date, and comment on the date's significance in either medieval or renaissance history. Opal must collect things: plants, animals, ribbons, poker chips. She must chant or repeat certain phrases, such as "the man who wears gray neckties and is kind to mice." She must count objects and actions (9 caterpillars, 12 baby chickens, 9 apron pleats, 3 pets for the pig, a vase breaks into 11 pieces, etc.). These rituals, repeated throughout the diary, are the threads that Opal stitches through the different patches. These rituals hold her world together. Thus the diary is unified, but by a different approach than a diarist might normally employ. The scraps become a sort of crazy quilt.

Characterization

Usually, when someone reads another person's diary, the reader gets to know the author's friends, family, and even enemies. But in the case of Opal's diary, the reader gets to know the animals in her life instead (though not all that well). Like other writers on the spectrum, such as Thoreau or Temple Grandin, Opal does not write about her siblings or her friends. Instead, she writes about the animals that matter most to her: her pets. The animals are only developed superficially: there is no depth to the development, and no knowledge of character or psychology is manifested.

The animals are domestic animals of the farm and wild creatures of the forest that she has observed, spent time with, and tamed. They are only identified by their names. The Opal of the diary has apparently read a great deal, because she is able to give them such names as Agamemnon and Aphrodite and Amadeus. The frontispiece of the edition of Opal's diary that was edited by Benjamin Hoff contains an alphabetical list of every animal that she gives a name to—the list is quite extensive.

Opal befriends the pigs in the pigpen, the family horse, the cow and her calf, the pigs, chickens, and the family dog. Out in the woods she befriends mice, rats, toads, crows, bats, and other small creatures. She creates elaborate little stories to go with some of the animals. The chicken, for example, gets a fancy outfit and a bonnet, and her chicks all get little christening gowns and ribbons for the christening ceremony Opal performs in the barn. One of the mice likes to ride around in Opal's pocket. So does a toad. Her pet crow likes to steal shiny things. The pig, who grunts her conversation, likes to walk to school with Opal.

By presenting these characters on a superficial level, Opal avoids the impossible task of figuring out human beings. The other humans she occasionally mentions—a woman who lives down the road, a man who works in the woods, her mother (whom she calls "the mama")—are not developed very well. The animals Opal writes about are similar to the fairies in Yeats's poems or the mermaids and princesses in Hans Christian Andersen's stories. They are interesting on the surface, but there is no depth to them. Since people with autism are prone to lack knowledge of other people's mental states, it would follow that it is very challenging for them to write about other people's mental states as well.

Themes

One of the unspoken themes hinted at in Opal's diary is the search for a sense of belonging. In the pages of her diary, Opal tries to figure out who she is, who her parents are, and where she fits in to the grand scheme of things. She develops the concept that her mother does not accept her as she is; in fact, "the mama" doesn't even seem to love her. She uses Opal as a babysitter for the smaller child, but otherwise is constantly shooing her out of the house. Opal does many things that are typical of children her age, but also does things one might more typically see a child with Asperger's Syndrome do: she fixates endlessly on forbidden things such as blue dye or mending glue or Vaseline and makes enormous messes for her mother to clean up. She obsesses about Catholic rituals and steals fabric and ribbons to make christening robes, burial shrouds, etc. for the animals she plays with. Her mother beats her for these strange behaviors and imprisons her under the bed. We never get an image of any family member hugging Opal or demonstrating love toward her. It's no wonder she searches for alternative "family" elsewhere. The other adult neighbors in the area become surrogate aunts and uncles for Opal. More importantly, the animals that she tames function as her family: she enjoys feeding them, bathing them, and taking care of them as she might her own children. Opal reminds us that animals make wonderful companions for children on the autism spectrum.

The theme of Opal's search for a sense of belonging parallels what we find in other life writings by authors on the spectrum. In *Nobody Nowhere*, Donna Williams recounts how she was a quirky child whose mother either neglected her or abused her throughout her childhood. Daniel Tammet was rejected by most of the other kids at school. Liane Holliday Willey found that she could not "fit in" with the other students at the university she attended. Temple Grandin's book *Emergence* describes a lifetime of feeling alienated from others.

On the flip side, Opal's childhood diary does celebrate the healing powers of nature. While she may not find a sense of belonging in society, she does find it in nature. In her emphasis on how nature can mend the heart and renew the spirit she resembles fellow American authors Emily Dickinson and Thoreau. All three writers had trouble relating to other people and preferred a quiet walk in the woods to a noisy social gathering.

Like Thoreau, Opal lived outdoors rather than indoors. Both had strong powers of sight and hearing and used them to take in their natural surroundings. Both patiently observed animals in the wild. Both tamed wild animals as pets. Both of them liked nothing more than a long tramp through the woods, alone. Like Dickinson, Opal also appreciated the plants she found around her. Both of them liked to garden. Both appreciated the beauty of flowers. Both of them liked to collect, identify, and classify specimens. Dickinson's herbarium and Opal's *Fairyland of Science* are similar.

Opal's diary can serve as a guidebook for other children on the autism spectrum. Her advice to them would surely be to find your strengths in life, celebrate what you know you can do well, and revel in the healing powers of nature. You don't have to follow the path that others take—if you find that you don't fit in, it's ok to blaze your own trail, your own way. It's good to create your own happiness.

Conclusion

Opal's diary has much to teach us about the natural world and our place in it. Her observations of mice and toads, her celebrations of trees and ferns and creeks, remind us that there is more to the world than we can find inside a house or office. Her diary also gives us great insight into the heart of a child. The observations she provides readers with carry us back to a time in our own lives when it was fun to play outside and fun to make-believe. Her writings remind us what it was like to feel a tooth wiggling, to walk barefoot in mud, and to cry at the loss of a pet. Her writings bring us joy:

> By-and-by, I came to a log. It was a nice little log. It was as long as three pigs as long as Peter Paul Reubens. I climbed upon it. I so did to look more looks about. The wind did blow in a real quick way—he made music all around. I danced on the log. It is so much a big amount of joy to dance on a log when the wind does play the harps in the forest. Then do I dance on tiptoe. I wave greetings to the plant-bush folks that do dance all about. Today a grand pine tree did wave its arms to me, and the bush branches patted my cheek in a friendly way. The wind again did blow back my curls—they clasped the fingers of the bush-people most near. I did turn around to untangle them. (143)

Significantly, her diary also reveals to the world the thought processes and feelings of a child on the autism spectrum, a child who grew up in a community that didn't understand, appreciate, or want her. We are lucky to have this written document that allows us to see the autistic child's perspective.

An informed, sympathetic reading of Opal's diary reveals the challenges that life-writing poses for someone on the autistic spectrum. The challenge of living in a hostile environment is met by the construction of alternative identities. The challenge of developing a cohesive narrative strategy is met by developing alternative narrative structures. And the seemingly impossible process of writing an original work is supplanted with the technique of braiding together previously read texts. There were times when Opal was very discouraged as a writer, but she kept her pen busy throughout her life. I was touched when I found in her papers an encouraging letter her grandmother had written to her when she was in college: "I think you will succeed...you have the determination and perseverance that makes success sure to those that are in love with their work" (University of Oregon Special Collections).

I am unable to understand the hostility with which many readers, critics, and even biographers have approached her work. I have found various degrees of sarcasm and condescension directed toward her and her diary. I think the hostility springs from a lack of understanding about her disability and how it affected her. But, after sharing her diary with a classroom full of sympathetic readers, I'm glad to know I'm not the only reader who recognizes the special message this text brings us as a manifestation of autism. It's no surprise that autistic readers and parents of children with autism have immensely enjoyed reading this diary, and have appreciated and celebrated her wonderful, quirky writing abilities just the way they are.

Works Cited

Beck, Katherine. *Opal: A Life of Enchantment, Mystery, and Madness.* New York: Penguin, 2003.

Belmonte, Matthew K. "Human, but More So: What the Autistic Brain Tells Us about the Process of Narrative." http://cwru.edu/affil/sce/Texts_2005/Autism%20and%20Representation%20Belmonte.htm. Forthcoming in *Autism and Representation.* Mark Osteen, ed. Oxford: Routledge, 2007. Used by permission.

Fortt, Inez. "The Education of an Understanding Heart." *The Call Number* [newsletter of the University of Oregon library], November 1956. University of Oregon Special Collections.

Hoff, Benjamin, ed. *The Singing Creek Where the Willows Grow: The Mystical Nature Diary of Opal Whiteley.* New York: Penguin, 1986 (all of my quotations from the diary are taken from this edition).

Letter from Grandma. Knight Library, University of Oregon Special Collections. Box 1, Folder 9. Used by permission.

Tammet, Daniel. *Born on a Blue Day: Inside the Extraordinary Mind of an Autistic Savant.* New York: Free Press, 2006.

Whiteley, Opal. *The Fairyland Around Us.* [Opal self-published this book, and copies are rare, but a copy of it can be found online] http://www.efn.org/%7Ecaruso/fairyland/canvas-preface-03.htm.

Williams, Donna. *Nobody Nowhere: The Extraordinary Autobiography of an Autistic.* New York: Avon, 1992.

CHAPTER TEN

Autistic Autobiography

Before Temple Grandin's ground-breaking autobiography *Emergence: Labeled Autistic* was published in 1986, the few non-fiction books about individuals with autism that did exist were either clinical studies written by professionals or biographies narrated by the subjects' mothers. Grandin led the way for other writers on the spectrum to follow—her book served as a guidepost for others on the autism spectrum who wished to write their own life stories. This chapter will examine the themes common to Grandin's book and four other autistic autobiographies. Looking closely at the autobiographical writings of people diagnosed with autism reveals a wealth of information about an autistic writer's motivation, use of genre convention, point of view, representation of self, content selection, themes, metaphors, and style.

An autistic autobiography occupies a unique place in literature. As an autobiography, of course, it fulfills the reader's expectations by providing a sustained narrative of the experiences of one individual based on his/her memories rather than research. It may reasonably be compared to a variety of sub-genres including the personal quest story, the *Bildungsroman*, the coming of age story, the women's memoir, the disability memoir, the gothic novel, or even the slave narrative. In recent years, the autistic autobiography has become its own genre with its own set of conventions and traditions.

Defining a New Genre

Grandin's groundbreaking work provided a sort of template for other authors on the spectrum to consider. Most of the autistic autobiographies that followed hers include several of the following elements:

- a dedication or thank you, usually to an important family member
- foreword or introduction, usually by a recognized expert in psychology
- an account of early childhood marked by troubling symptoms of autism spectrum disorders, especially sensory sensitivities, sensory overload, communication problems, uncontrollable behaviors, and withdrawal from the world
- an account of adolescence with increased feelings of anxiety, isolation, and alienation
- at some point in the narrative, the diagnosis
- after the diagnosis, an emphasis on education, training, medication, therapy
- a special parent, friend, teacher, or counselor who gives moral support and encouragement
- an account of adulthood, gradually progressing toward self-understanding, more satisfying relationships, greater independence, continued education, and work
- a need to find and connect with other adults on the spectrum
- suggestions, helpful hints, instructions for the reader
- bibliography for suggested reading.

It must be noted here that this book of Grandin's, and others by her, were written in conjunction with a co-author. It would be interesting to know more about what the shared writing process was like for them and how it shaped the finished product. Grandin's co-author, Margaret Scariano, seemed to have edited the work with a neurotypical audience in mind. This would parallel the way autobiographies written by slaves in the American South were often edited by Northern white editors who then disseminated the polished stories to a sympathetic white audience—we should be grateful that the authors were given this kind of help in order to "get the word out," yet we may also sadly wonder about the richness of authentic language and storytelling that must have been lost in the process. Herman Melville knew that he was writing for two different audiences—himself and the world—and he struggled to please both, ultimately feeling frustrated by the process: "What I feel most moved to write, that is banned—it will not pay. Yet, altogether, write the *other* way I cannot. So the product is a final hash, and all my books are botches" (Bellis 83).

Psychologist Francesca Happé has argued that individuals with autism are not able to write their autobiographies without some kind of assistance. Dawn Prince-Hughes sums up Happé's argument thusly: "the most coherent, most relevant and revealing autobiographies of people on the autistic spectrum are of dubious value as they are, by necessity, edited with a heavy hand—even translated, if you will—by 'normal' people who end up making the work mostly their own" (*Aquamarine Blue 5* xii). As a scholar who has not only written an autobiography but has also collected other "personal stories" by autistics into an anthology (*Aquamarine Blue 5*), Prince-Hughes is in "substantial disagreement" with this theory. The other authors in this study have written their autobiographies without this kind of assistance.

Diagnosis as Turning Point

Central to the five autobiographies in this study is the diagnosis, which is narrated as a climactic moment in the subject's life and becomes a turning point in his/her personal development. The diagnosis not only changes the way the author feels about him or herself, but also changes the way the reader feels about the author: the author's claims to be autistic are legitimized, giving the story more validity and value. Readers with autism will thus be able to identify more closely with the author's struggles and learn about people like them; neurotypical readers will be able to learn more about people who experience the world differently.

Grandin's diagnosis presents itself in the subtitle: "Labeled Autistic." The introduction reinforces the fact with "I was labeled autistic" and "I was evaluated as being autistic" (8). Grandin's mother was very aggressive in seeking medical and psychological help for her daughter, and the early diagnosis made it possible for her mother to enlist several professionals (nanny, speech therapist, tutors, and private schools) to help her daughter grow and flourish. In the autobiography, establishing the diagnosis first, before telling the story, adds poignancy to Grandin's earliest memories and bravado to her struggle toward a normal and totally independent adulthood.

Other autobiographies followed suit. In 1992, Donna Williams's autobiography *Nobody Nowhere* chronicled the story of an Australian woman who sought out her own diagnosis as a young adult in order to understand who she was and why life was so hard for her. In her early twenties, desperate for self-knowledge, she bought a second-hand typewriter and hammered out everything she knew about herself, which became the first draft of her autobiography. She took her manuscript to a mental health professional and demanded an answer: "I've written a book. I want you to read it and tell me why I'm like I am" (188). The diagnosis of autism brought her relief and a feeling of closure: "The [autobiography] was finished and now I had a word for the problem I had fought to overcome and understand...it helped me to forgive myself and my family for the way I was" (192). That word was *autism.* Armed with this diagnosis, Williams went on to research autism and to become an advocate for people on the spectrum. She went on to write three more volumes of her autobiography and numerous self-help books.

In 1999 Liane Holliday Willey published *Pretending to be Normal*, about her journey through life with Asperger's Syndrome (AS). As a child Willey sensed she was different from others, but it wasn't until she faced overwhelming obstacles in college that she realized that she had sensory, cognitive, and social challenges that her college peers did not have. Her own diagnosis followed the diagnosis of her AS daughter, and once again a sense of relief and closure followed: "I had finally reached the end of my race to be normal. And that was exactly what I needed. A finish—an end to the pretending that had kept me running in circles for most of my life" (112). Like Grandin and Williams, Willey educated herself about autism and Asperger's Syndrome and became an advocate for not only herself and her daughter, but for others on the spectrum. The final chapter of her book is filled with helpful information for others who struggle as she has.

In Dawn Prince-Hughes' autobiography *Songs of the Gorilla Nation* (2004) the diagnosis was sought after an important relationship reached a roadblock. Prince-Hughes and her partner needed to understand the dynamics of their relationship as Prince-Hughes's mounting anxiety was frequently giving way to bursts of depression or bad temper. A nephew's diagnosis of Asperger's Syndrome pointed her in the right direction—in typical Aspergen fashion she researched the syndrome, created complex charts and narratives, compiled interviews of family members, and edited videotapes from her childhood. Armed with this evidence, Prince-Hughes marched into a professional's office and announced, "I need a diagnosis of Asperger's Syndrome" (173). When she read the official diagnosis soon after, she too experienced relief and closure: "I felt an immense wave of relief wash over me as everything suddenly made sense... It made me feel both better and worse knowing that I hadn't meant to disturb or hurt anyone" (174).

The diagnosis divides the "before" (what's wrong with me?) from the "after" (what do I do now?). In all cases, the subject is relieved by the diagnosis and finds closure to a troubling feeling that "something wasn't quite right." The diagnosis also helps the author to gain insight and to define the self more clearly, which allows the author to build stronger relationships to others, both neurotypical and autistic.

Liquid Identity/Slippery Language

Writers on the spectrum face two challenges when sitting down to write an autobiography, both of them caused by the nature of autism itself. One problem is that the concept of "self" is not always so neatly defined in the autistic psyche. The other problem is that communication through the art form's medium—language—is an inherent part of the disability. While the process of writing an autobiography can be daunting for anyone, it is especially challenging for people who are not comfortable defining who they are through language. But when a person with autism does record his/her life story on paper, readers are richly rewarded with the opportunity to learn more about the human heart and its longing to be understood by others.

The authors in this study all write about a fluidity of boundary between different parts of the self, between the self and the physical world outside, and also between the self and other people. As these authors journeyed from "no self" to "self," they tried on a number of alternate identities along the way. It's as though they needed to develop their personality traits separately at first, and then fuse them later on into one coherent whole. Fitzgerald similarly observes that "those with Asperger's Syndrome…have a poor sense of identity or self. As a result, they are often engaged in a constant search for identity and may adopt multiple roles or reinvent themselves in some way—something known as identity diffusion" (*Autism* 16). All five of the autobiographies in this chapter chronicle the process of creating multiple selves before fusing them into one whole coherent self. During the period when the identity is still forming, the author's use of language is experimental, playful, and variable according to the situation. The process of writing the story down helps the writer to make sense of the process of identity construction: "their artistic work is an effort to sort out their confused identities" (Fitzgerald *Genesis* 239).

Donna Williams's identity was in constant flux as she was growing up. As a severely autistic young girl she didn't have a sense of herself as an individual person. She seemed to exist, rather, as a bundle of sensory impressions. Her story recorded the sensory stimulus, but not the physical, cognitive, or emotional response. Her earliest memories included staring into bright lights, being fascinated by color and shine, losing herself in texture, hearing voices but not comprehending language, and feeling pain but not understanding the fist that delivered it. She was confused by "the world" out there: "The world seemed to be impatient, annoying, callous, and unrelenting. I learned to respond to it as such, crying, squealing, ignoring it, and running away" (4).

Williams eventually came to realize that the moving, yelling, pain-inflicting beings around her were people. People came in two types: the ones she liked to be near (a kind aunt, her father), and the ones she avoided (an abusive mother, her brother). Gradually she came to realize that she was a person as well. By the time Williams was three, she pulled herself together and coped with the painful confusion around her by becoming "Willie," a tough little boy who could somehow manage the painful and confusing world around him:

> Willie became the self I directed at the outside world, complete with hateful glaring eyes, a pinched-up mouth, a rigid corpselike stance, and clenched fists. Willie stamped his foot, Willie spat when he didn't like things, but the look of complete hatred was the worst weapon and Donna paid the price. (11)

When Williams was about four, she took on another identity, "Carol," named for a nice girl she met one day in the park. From that point on, Williams would "become Carol" any time she wanted to show a friendly, congenial self to the outside world:

> Carol was everything that people liked. Carol laughed a lot. Carol made friends. Carol brought things home. Carol had a mother. To my mother's delight, Carol could act relatively normal. (19)

Throughout the autobiography, Williams' identity remained fluid. The "I" point of view remained that of Donna: the main character, the protagonist, the narrator. And yet the two other central characters appeared to take the wheel from Donna when they were needed. When Donna faced a difficult situation, either Willie stepped forward on Donna's behalf to fight for her, or Carol appeared to smooth things over and make everything ok. Years later, as an adult, Donna was able to say goodbye to both Willie and Carol, deciding that she could on her own summon the skills needed to interact with people in the world. She remained grateful, however, for having had them in her life: "I would never have been able to develop my intellect [without] the character of Willie [or] my ability to communicate [without] the character of Carol" (200).

As a girl, her relationship to language was problematic. In her website, Donna explains that "around two thirds of people diagnosed with autism don't develop verbal language and around one third develop language which remains highly idiosyncratic or 'dysfunctional'. I was in this second group, able to speak but not having fluent functional language until late childhood" (donnawilliams.net). Like many other people with autism, Williams' language acquisition was delayed. Several psychologists have explored the relationship between delayed language acquisition and delayed concept of self. In order to understand who we are, we must use language to narrate stories about ourselves. Jean Quigley summarizes the research of several people: "not only does narrative provide privileged focus for examining the culture of language, but there may also be a special affinity between narrative and self, such that narratives can be said to play a special role in the process of self-construction" (quoted by Fitzgerald *Autism* 46).

In *Nobody Nowhere,* Williams shared her journey through the changing landscape of language. Her earliest memories were of hearing words but not understanding them. The command "Stop it!", incomprehensible to Williams, would be followed with a *slap.* Soon Williams began a phase of echolalia, repeating the commands in an attempt to demonstrate some kind of compliance. She would hear "Don't repeat everything I say" and answer with "Don't repeat everything I say," which would also be followed with a *slap.* As she grew older she tried on different voices—for six months she used an American accent that irritated a teacher she disliked. Even as an adult Williams could not seem to settle on just one voice:

> I would often fluctuate between accents and pitches and would vary the manner in which I described things. Sometimes my accent seemed quite polished and refined. Sometimes I spoke as though I was born and bred in the gutter. Sometimes my pitch was normal, at other times it was deep, like I was doing an Elvis impersonation. When I was excited, however, it sounded like Mickey Mouse after being run over by a steamroller—high pitched and flat. (84)

The dramatic range of voices was a problem for her when she worked at a department store, but was more welcome when she worked in a theater costume shop.

Like many other people with autism, Williams retreated from the language of others but compensated by creating a new communication system that she could understand. "I developed a language of my own," she wrote. "Everything I did, from holding two fingers together to scrunching up my toes, had a meaning" (29). She was trying to tell people how she felt, but they only saw her symbols as another manifestation of "mad Donna" and ignored her or, worse, ridiculed her.

Written language posed a challenge for Williams as well: "I could understand individual words, but understanding written sentences was as hard as understanding heard ones. They just ended up in a meaningless tumble" (donnawilliams.net). Williams dropped out of several schools as she was growing up, and by the time she reached college she was placed into a remedial writing course. Mechanics such as capitalization and punctuation were baffling for her—she used the marks either randomly or in relation to her own thought process, but not as a tool to help the reader. When writing a personal narrative, she once used the pronoun "you" instead of "I," which prompted the teacher to ask, "is this some kind of joke?" After finishing a composition she would draw a picture over the top of it before handing it in. Once she recycled a sheet of paper by covering the entire page with correction fluid and then writing over the top of the crusty surface. By sheer tenacity and stubbornness, Williams improved her writing skills little by little and was able to graduate from the university. As an adult, Williams is currently a talented, best-selling author, poet, and songwriter who is able to support herself through her writing projects.

Prince-Hughes, like Williams, lacked a clear sense of self as a young child. Looking back, she recalled how "my parents were often frustrated with me because I would 'walk through' or 'look through' people as if they weren't there. This phenomenon had more to do with my unawareness of where my body began and ended than with awareness of other people's boundaries… I myself had no such edges" (29). Prince-Hughes eventually created "edges" for herself by trying on several identities one by one, including primitive girl in the woods, exotic dancer, lesbian biker, gorilla, scholar, and finally partner and mother. Over time these layers of identity fused together into the woman who wrote the autobiography.

The most interesting and unusual identity that Prince-Hughes explored was "gorilla." Meeting the gorillas at the Seattle Zoo was a life-altering experience for her—her autobiography explained that her relationship with the gorillas brought her closer to a primitive self that she thought had been lost to her. She was startled by how similar her autistic self was to her gorilla self:

> I went forward by going backward. I went backward in time into the most primal and ancient part of myself. Back into the quiet recesses of the mind, where evolution has paused to breathe, bringing its people with it. I did this with the first and best friends I ever had: a family of captive gorillas, people of an ancient nation. (3)

For four years, Prince-Hughes spent as much time as possible with "her people." She volunteered at the zoo, found employment there, and observed the gorillas with amazing perceptiveness and wisdom. Her job was to care for them, and in doing so she quickly grew to love them and identify with them. She shared their food, and sometimes she would crawl into their nests, smelling their gorilla smells, and feeling completely at home. Prince-Hughes' gorilla identity did not fade away with time—years later she still feels strongly connected to them, as though they have become her adopted family or tribe.

Growing up, Prince-Hughes learned to speak by following the same route Williams followed. Fortunately, her family was patient with her slow acquisition of language as she tested first words then phrases. Prince-Hughes was dazzled by interesting words as a little girl and would endlessly repeat things such as "hippopotamus" or "sssssilver dollar." She progressed to phrases by echoing what other people said to her, and over time she was able to try phrases and sentences on her own.

Prince-Hughes learned to speak the language of gorillas. She was able to communicate with them in a meaningful way, something few other people had been able to do. She felt a deep kinship with them, noticing that their perseveration, intense concentration, attention to detail, love of ritual, and stereotyped gestures were much like hers as a person with autism. She took great comfort from this, concluding: "Perhaps my own way of being is a very old way of being, a gift from my forebears" (148). She was patient enough to sit and observe and listen. She learned to interpret their gestures, facial expressions, and sounds. Her gorilla identity was so fixed that when she was introduced to a bonobo named Kanzi, he interacted with her briefly, observed her mannerisms, and then signed: "*you...gorilla...question*?" and continued to call her "gorilla" during their visit together.

Prince-Hughes's language development paralleled the development of her identity. She "tried on" different ways of speaking the same way she tried on different selves. She felt most comfortable speaking gorilla because they were the people she loved best. By the time Prince-Hughes became a mother, she was in control of both her language and herself. The closing remarks of her autobiography show how powerful a person's language can be toward creating harmony not only within oneself, but also in others:

> Autism is a way of sensing the world—the whole world—of creating and knowing. It is my hope that as more autistic people find places to *learn about themselves and grow, as they tell their stories for themselves and all people*, they will find ways to share their special talents with the world. (224, emphasis added)

This willingness to learn more about herself and to help others provides her with the motivation to write her life story down on paper.

Daniel Tammet was more interested in numbers than in words, more attracted to equations than sentences. Growing up, he seemed to be surer of himself than Williams or Prince-Hughes were. Like the others, he also embraced alternative identities that were quite different from what we might expect. One of his alter-egos was Anne, a female persona who would appear to him at the playground during recess. When writing his autobiography, Tammet could recall exactly what she looked like:

> She was a very tall woman, more than six feet in height, and covered from head to toe in a long, blue cloak. Her face was

> very thin and creased with wrinkles, because she was very, very old—more than a hundred years of age. Her eyes were like narrow, watery slits and they were often closed as if deep in thought. (78)

Her character was highly defined in his imagination—she was a widow whose husband had been a blacksmith, she had no children, and she enjoyed talking about philosophy. She was a good listener, and she did not think Daniel was strange (unlike the other children running around the playground). She even shared his eccentric interests: ladybugs, coin towers, numbers, books, and trees. Daniel cried when she told him it was time to say goodbye and part forever. Though he was not aware at the time, as an adult Daniel came to realize that she was actually a manifestation of another part of himself: "Anne was the personification of my feelings of loneliness and uncertainty. She was a product of that part of me that wanted to engage with my limitations and begin to break free of them. In letting her go, I was making the painful decision to try to find my way in the wider world and to live in it" (80).

Daniel Tammet was diagnosed with Asperger's Syndrome as well as Savant Syndrome, and his sense of self was stronger than some of the other authors studied here. The first chapters of his autobiography discuss his birth and early childhood years, but there is no discussion of how he developed spoken language. As a child he did enter into conversations, but he describes them as being very one-sided, with Daniel talking non-stop about his special interests until the other child would get tired of listening and walk away. All aspects of conversation—initiating conversation, introducing a topic, back and forth sharing, and listening to others—were nearly impossible for Tammet as he was growing up. Over time he was able to master these skills, and currently maintains happy and successful relationships with family, a partner, and friends.

When Tammet was young he was fascinated by the Phoenician alphabet, and would write his favorite words in Phoenician all over the garden shed. He loved to read the daily newspaper and report to his parents every spelling and grammatical error he found. By age eight he started to write stories, "often writing for hours at a time, covering sheet after sheet of paper with tightly knit words" (44). Tammet records that the stories had no emotions, character development, or dialogue. Instead, they were descriptions of colors, shapes, and textures, highly detailed but with no story to tie them together. This trait of favoring description over narrative and setting over character seems to come naturally to writers on the spectrum.

Alienation and its Metaphors

The most pronounced thread running through all five autobiographies is the theme of alienation. In all cases the authors explain how they knew they were different from their peers, and how that difference led to feelings of rejection, loneliness, isolation, frustration, and despair. As a child, the autistic subject is so wholly engrossed in himself that he "tunes out" the outside world and doesn't realize he is different. Around age ten or so, the author begins to notice the role of self in relation to peers, and this is when the feelings of difference start to surface. When the author engages in autistic behaviors in a public setting, usually school, the other children, teenagers, or adults respond in a variety of ways ranging from amusement to scorn to revulsion. The author's response is to feel alienation, which is best understood through metaphor. The metaphor serves two purposes: it helps the author to understand his or her own feelings, and it helps the neurotypical reader to gain an understanding of what it feels like to have autism.

Temple Grandin recalled having virtually no friends in middle school or high school. Because of her odd speech, unpredictable behavior, and lack of social savvy, the other kids taunted her, calling her "retard," "tape recorder," and "buzzard woman." Grandin knew she had many valuable qualities to share with a potential friend, but remembered how "in spite of my creative talents, I lacked the ability of getting along with people...they didn't warm to my erratic behavior, my stressed way of talking, my bizarre ideas, my jokes and tricks" (59). Grandin developed the metaphor of a "glass door" between her and the outside world to gain understanding of how her autism allowed her to see other people but not embrace them. Doors became important tropes in her story. She first pondered the concept of the door when she heard the pastor of her church talking about the door to heaven. But as she continued to think about doors, they came to represent barriers between her and all of the things she desired (self-knowledge, comfort, friendship, education), and since the barriers were glass, the objects were within sight but not within reach. In several instances she used the metaphor of the door to explain how isolated she felt from other people:

> I decided that getting along with people was like a sliding glass door. The door has to be approached slowly; it cannot be forced; otherwise, it will break. Relationships with people are the same way. If they are forced, the relationship doesn't work. One little shove can shatter everything. (120)

Each door was initially closed to her, but as she grew and matured she was able to open one door after another. The doors were then transformed into symbols of opportunity and personal empowerment. After Grandin earned her B.A. in psychology, her mother commemorated the achievement by giving her a golden charm engraved with the words "Through the Little Door."

Like Grandin, Dawn Prince-Hughes also felt alienated as she was growing up. Her school experiences were even worse than Grandin's. She was ridiculed and taunted, once called a "fucking freak of nature" by another girl, and Prince-Hughes was also physically and sexually abused and even tortured by her fellow schoolmates. She described several incidents of violence in her autobiography:

> People would corner me in the bathroom and force my head into the toilet, slam me in the head with books and spit on me. They defaced my locker. They took my food away. Once some

> senior students made a sign with a derogatory word on it and hung it around my neck. I didn't take it off. (60)

Only once did she respond physically—she jumped over a desk and tried to grab one of her tormenters—and for this she was expelled from school. Her usual defense was to try to ignore what was happening to her, and to internalize it. She became overwhelmed by anxiety and depression. In her autobiography, years later, she was able to gain some perspective to what was happening to her and could give her feelings language: "As I look back over the painful years I spent alienated, different, disconnected, and hurting, it's hard to understand how I made it" (27).

Like Grandin, Prince-Hughes created a metaphor for understanding her situation. As an adult, Prince-Hughes became interested in the gorillas at the zoo. As she watched the visitors who teased and heckled the gorillas, she identified with the animals, not the humans: "Autistic people can be left behind, hunted and haunted, looking through an often opaque glass." She contemplated how the glass wall that enclosed the gorilla's cage resembled the autism that enclosed her: "I am always aware of a moving sort of glass between me and the world," she said, eventually realizing that "I found a way to go home through the glass—the glass of my reality as an autistic person... I knew the glass was moving when a gorilla touched me. A gorilla touched me, and I connected to a living person [i.e. gorilla] as I had never done before" (5).

Just as Grandin's doors changed from barriers to gateways, so did Prince-Hughes's perspective on the glass gorilla cage change—from prison to sanctuary. As a volunteer and later an employee of the zoo, she gained entrance into the gorillas' world and was deeply moved by the experience of touching, smelling, and being near the gorillas, whom she considered to be her people. She realized that her autism had given her special gifts that allowed her to study and understand gorilla behavior. At the same time that she was visiting the gorillas, she was also experiencing tremendous personal growth as she graduated from college, found a life partner, and became a mother. Through education and medication she was able to control the symptoms of autism that were a problem for her, and she also grew to embrace the qualities of autism that she felt were her special gifts. Her autobiography described this change of perspective: "sometimes I feel like I am now the one in the zoo. Like any good gorilla chained by what is often unpleasant circumstance, I have evolved to incorporate endurance as a keystone" (177).

"I was, as far as I can make out, born alienated from the world," Donna Williams recalled in her autobiography *Nobody Nowhere.* Williams was rejected by most of her school-age peers but, more heartbreakingly, she was also rejected by her family. Her mother and older brother, especially, heaped abuse and scorn upon her almost from the time she was born. She was different from them and they couldn't understand her, so they humiliated and shamed her at every opportunity. In one instance her mother filled Williams's mouth with food and a large dishrag—the girl choked and was nearly killed. Her response, her way of coping with the abuse, was to withdraw further and further from "the world," finding sanctuary in "her world" of smell, touch, and sound.

Williams also referred to glass as a metaphor for alienation (*"In a world under glass, you can watch the world pass, and nobody can touch you, you think you are safe"*), but she developed the metaphor of the mirror as well. As a young girl she became fascinated by mirrors, sitting for hours peering into them, wondering about the "other girl," an alter-ego she named Carol. Williams longed to enter Carol's world because it looked calmer and more peaceful than the one she inhabited. She repeatedly threw her body into the mirror, hoping to fall through it, as Alice did into her looking-glass. Williams explained how the mirrored world was the reverse image of her own world, just as an autistic person's way of seeing things can be quite different from a neurotypical's. Strangely, when Williams was under a good deal of stress, her neurology somehow conspired against her to change her physical world into a fun-house manifestation of its reverse image: she actually did see everything in reverse for a few days:

> One day I left a building through the same door I had come in, yet I found that somehow the building had changed places. It was not on the same side of the street as before. I walked back into the building, turning my back on the street outside, then I walked back out again. It was still opposite from the way it had been when I had originally gone in... I began to cry; I was afraid... The whole world seemed to have turned itself upside down, inside out, and back to front. Everything was like a mirror image of what it had been when I had entered the building... This happened on and off for two days. I became terribly afraid that I had gone mad. (156–157)

As Williams came to know herself better, she eventually pulled herself away from the world she found in the mirror. When she was diagnosed and finally understood that she was an autistic person, she read everything she could find about autism in order to learn more about who she was. She started to study sociology and psychology in college to learn more about herself in relation to others. She bought a used typewriter and hammered out an autobiography in a search for self-understanding. It hurt to enter the real world—it was scary to leave her old self behind—but it was what she wanted, and in the end she found the strength she needed to overcome many of her autistic traits. "I was bathing in the freedom to be me," she says, "I had a solid sense of home and belonging in my own body" (192). No longer did she stare at the mirror for hours wishing to be that other girl—she realized that the girl she was would be ok.

Liane Holliday Willey grew up in a more tolerant, understanding environment. Her parents recognized that she was different, but accepted her quirkiness and challenged her to grow and develop in her own way. She lived in a small town, and the other children at school included her in activities and did not ostracize her. Willey pointed out that it wasn't until she reached college that her differences created significant problems for her. She suffered from two basic problems in college—one was a problem with logistics, such as finding classrooms, remembering schedules, solving problems, and processing sensory information. The large university was simply too overwhelming. The other problem was social—she could not make a friend, could not fit into a group, and could not work effectively with other students. The first problem made college more difficult than it should have been. The second problem was an assault to her self-respect: "my differences were not just superficial incidentals, but cracks in my dignity" (51).

Holliday Willey invented several metaphors to describe her autistic alienation—all of them of a spatial nature: "I was an outsider," "I had been tossed aside," "the gap widened," "losing my way," "a slow walk home," feeling "locked out," and eventually "crossing the bridge." Willey did not favor one controlling metaphor for her writing, like Grandin, Prince-Hughes, and Williams; rather, she created a new one for each situation. Still, each one was an expression of the distance or barriers between herself and "normal" people. She ends her story with the metaphor of crossing a bridge, which is a hopeful way of talking about how self-knowledge gives way to self-love, which gives way to an ability to love others and connect with them.

Daniel Tammet's autobiography recounts that he was not interested in other children when he was young. He had no memories of playing with others at school, but he did remember fondly the enjoyment he felt from spinning coins on a hard surface. At home he did not feel connected to his siblings, but he was strongly connected to his parents' books. This preference for things over people is typical of young autistic or AS children. As Tammet grew older and started to reach out to the people around him, they often rejected him because he was different: "I am ten and know that I am different to them in a way that I cannot express or comprehend... it is perceived as common knowledge that Daniel talks to the trees and that he is weird" (73). Eventually, a feeling of alienation set in: "There was certainly no shortage of times when I felt like I wanted to vanish. I just did not seem to fit in anywhere as though I had been born into the wrong world. The sense of never feeling quite comfortable or secure, of always being somehow apart and separate, weighed heavily on me" (74).

Although relationships with other people proved to be challenging, Tammet was able to find satisfaction and pleasure by immersing himself in numbers and mathematics. His love-affair with numbers began at a very young age:

> For as long as I can remember, I have experienced numbers in the visual, synesthetic way that I do. Numbers are my first language, one I often think and feel in. Emotions can be hard for me to understand or know how to react to, so I often use numbers to help me. If a friend says they feel sad or depressed, I picture myself sitting in the dark hollowness of number 6 to help me experience the same sort of feeling and understand it. If I read in an article that a person felt intimidated by something, I imagine myself standing next to the number 9...by doing this, numbers actually help me get closer to understanding other people. (7)

Tammet's synesthesia gave him the ability to see the numbers in his head—each number had a specific, unique shape and color. When young Tammet spent hours and days looking at his parents' books, he wasn't reading the words, he was looking at the page numbers, which meant a lot more to him than story.

Not surprisingly, his metaphor for understanding his autistic self was not glass or mirrors, but numbers. The numbers he liked best were prime numbers: "I can recognize every prime up to 9973 by their 'pebble-like' quality. It's just the way my brain works," he explained (1). Like people with autism, prime numbers are rare and sometimes hard to identify. Like people with autism, prime numbers are unique and beautiful and very special. Tammet devoted several pages of his autobiography to the discussion of prime numbers, which he clearly saw as the "building blocks" of his numerical world. The language he used when describing them made it clear that he saw them as metaphors for autistic people: "Each one is so different from the one before and the one after. Their loneliness among the other numbers makes them so conspicuous and interesting to me" (9).

But Tammet's favorite number, the one that signaled his wish to join society in a meaningful way, was pi. Like a person with autism spectrum disorder, pi shows up in all sorts of unexpected places: "it occurs in the distribution of primes and in the probability that a pin dropped on a set of parallel lines intersects a line. Pi also appears as the average ratio of the actual length and direct distance between source and mouth of a meandering river" (174). One day when Tammet's father called and reminded him that it had been 20 years since his last epileptic seizure, Tammet decided to celebrate this milestone by organizing a fund-raiser to benefit epilepsy research. He decided to raise money by breaking the world's record for memorizing the most digits of pi—at Oxford University he ended up reciting perfectly, from memory, 22,514 places (if only Lewis Carroll had been there to witness the feat). When people asked him why he wanted to memorize so many pi digits, he compared pi to a Mozart symphony or the Mona Lisa: "[it] is an extremely beautiful and utterly unique thing...pi is its own reason for loving it" (185). The symbolic value of the number became even clearer as it morphed into a landscape in a dream: "I fell asleep and dreamed that I was walking among my pi number landscapes—there at least I felt calm and confident" (181).

The metaphors created by these authors to represent their autism—glass doors, glass cages, mirrors, spatial barriers, and prime numbers—may be viewed positively or negatively. The authors in this study are more likely to use the negative aspects of the metaphor before their diagnosis: the door that is closed, the cage that confines, the number that cannot contain other numbers, and so on. But after the diagnosis has been reached and the author moves toward a greater understanding of autism and its meaning in the individual's life, the metaphor is used as a happier manifestation of the autistic self—the door becomes a portal to a new future, a cage becomes a refuge of safety, a ravine is bridged, and prime numbers sparkle with uniqueness and beauty.

The Search for Others like Me

There is no better cure for alienation than companionship. And there is no better companion than someone who not only understands me but also has something in common with me. The most alienated character in all literature, perhaps, was Frankenstein's monster, a deformed man who resembled no other on the planet and was thus cruelly rejected by every person he encountered. Realizing that he was doomed to a life of rejection and aloneness, he pleaded with his maker, Victor Frankenstein, to create for him a partner—someone who was just like him and who was also different from the rest of the world: "I am alone and miserable; man will not associate with me," he wailed, arguing for a partner. "My companion must be of the same species and have the same defects. This being you must create" (Shelley 137).

In a similar vein, Donna Williams understood that she was different from her family and from others in their neighborhood and that this is why she was continually rejected. When her younger brother Tom was born, however, she quickly perceived that he was "like her," and this created a special kinship bond between them. She was able to make eye contact with him (and *only* him), and even when he was an infant she felt that "he was on [her] side" (27). He shared Williams's musical giftedness, sensitivity to light and color, and difficulty with language. She understood the world he moved in and felt closer to him than other family members.

After she was diagnosed with autism, she set out in search of other autistics: "I wanted to meet the other autistic people I'd been told about and was surprised to find out that they were few and far between, scattered across the country and across the world... Now it was time to meet people still trapped in the place I had come from and in some ways was still in" (193).

Bryn was one such person, a young man Williams met while in college. He was as quiet and non-communicative as she was, but they found that they could still understand each other's thoughts and feelings. They found non-verbal ways to show their affection, such as sharing food or brushing each other's hair. For nearly a year they maintained close ties while attending classes. Eventually the stress of such an emotional entanglement proved too much for Williams at that time, and she found it necessary to abandon their relationship, though she still had warm feelings for him. Williams's other autobiographies (she has written a series of four books) chronicle a series of friendships, romances, and marriages to other autistic people. These people are Williams's emotional support system and have become her tribe.

Tammet's brothers and sisters all seem to display shadow traits of autism spectrum disorder, and his brother Steven has been diagnosed with Asperger's Syndrome. Tammet recognizes some of his own behaviors in his brother, such as the need to walk in circles, a fondness for encyclopedic knowledge, and an obsession with special interests. Tammet's affection for this brother is obvious: "[Steven] is a very gentle and caring person, and I am proud of him and very hopeful about his future" (217).

Daniel Tammet's meeting with fellow autistic-savant Kim Peek (on whom the film *Rain Man* was based) proved to be one of the highlights of both of their lives. The visit was arranged by a documentary film crew, and their meeting took place at the Salt Lake City Public Library. "This was to be a moment I had long waited for; it would be the first time in my life that I had met and spoken with another savant" (200). The two men were able to communicate with each other as they could with almost nobody else in the world. The conversation included discussions of calendar dates and days, statistics and zip codes, numbers, and their love of learning. On the way home, Tammet reflected back on his experience of finding another person like him: "Kim and I had much in common, but most important of all was the sense of connection I think we both felt during our time together. Our lives had in many ways been very different and yet somehow we shared this special, rarefied bond... Meeting Kim Peek was one of the happiest moments of my life" (203).

As a child, Willey seemed to be unaware of how different she was from other children, but as a college student she felt it acutely and yearned to find "someone like me" (52). Several years later, it came as a welcome relief to Willey to finally understand that she and her daughter both had a neurological basis for their differences from the other family members. Although Willey enjoyed a loving, close relationship with her husband and all of her children, the AS daughter seemed to capture her heart in a special way:

> I was different. So was my little girl. Different, challenged even, but not bad or unable or incorrect. I understood my husband's tears and his fear for our daughter's future, but I did not relate to them. I knew my innate understanding of what the world of AS is like would help my daughter make her way through life. Together, we would find every answer either of us ever needed. (112)

The dual diagnosis was a moment of rebirth for Willey. Armed with a clearer picture of who she was, she could become a better mother for her daughter, and they could enjoy a special bond, a special closeness, and a special means of communication. They seemed to read each other's thoughts and could communicate with only a glance or small gesture. Willey reports that when something interesting or annoying or frustrating happens, a glance to the daughter reveals a mutual understanding of what is happening as well as a mutually shared reaction: "As soon as I sense my daughter's thoughts, I look to her and am never surprised to see her looking back at me with a *You see what I see, don't you mom?* expression in her eyes" (114).

Autistic individuals, as a minority group, can have a hard time finding each other since they are not linked through geography or gender or appearance. One of the happy by-products of writing and publishing autobiographies such as these is that the book becomes an agent of meeting other individuals with autism from around the world. These authors have appeared on television, gone on speaking tours, been featured at conferences, and are asked to advocate in countless ways for individuals on the spectrum. Their continued work brings other autistics together as well, and for this we should all be grateful.

Motivation for Writing

The decision for anyone to write a life story is probably motivated by a complex combination of factors. There seem to be two primary reasons why the authors in this study have put their life stories onto the page and into the bookstores in the world.

Like all writers, the author of an autistic autobiography wants to make sense of his or her life, and to give it meaning. Research tells us that people on the spectrum are poor at providing overall coherence to information due to weakened executive function, but good at retaining detailed, specific memories. "[Autistic] writers have huge problems in what Jean Quigley (2000) calls 'self-construction'. Paradoxically, these massive struggles can help them in their creative literary works. They have to construct deliberately what comes automatically for neurotypicals (non-autistic people)" (Fitzgerald *Genesis* 28). The act of recalling memories and organizing them into one narrative can be a satisfying project like tracing lines between stars to form constellations. The opening paragraph of Willey's chapter emphasizes this point:

> Looking back does not mean I will go backward. Remembering can teach me who I am and guide me toward who I will be. Remembering can set me free... I like being able to revisit my past, but only when I bring along a measure of clinical behaviorism... I simply use my past as a catalyst for conscious thought and for self-appreciation. (17)

Prince-Hughes, who started writing her thoughts down around five years old, notes that "writing was my salvation" and that writing brought her "a peaceful world of art and order, a land we can share" (26). Currently a professor of social sciences, she brings an anthropologist's perspective to her own autobiography in order to understand her culture of one as well as how it relates to the majority culture around her. Tammet also gives this motivation for writing down his life story: "Writing about my life has given me the opportunity to get some perspective on just how far I've come, and to trace the arc of my journey up to the present" (12).

Many writers on the spectrum express the hope that committing their life story to paper, and having that story validated through publication and publicity, will add meaning to their lives. As Prince-Hughes comments, "Adults with autism long to see their experiences related and validated by others" (7). Other adults with autism may seek this same kind of validation through relationships, through meaningful employment, through hobbies, or through other creative talents such as music, painting, or drama. Temple Grandin knows she will not marry or have children. For Grandin, her work with animals, her feedlot designs, and her writing projects will live on after her and thus give her a measure of immortality.

A second motivation for writing the autistic memoir is the hope that such a project will help others to understand more about autism: both helping people with autism understand more about themselves and also helping neurotypicals understand the autistic people in their lives. This is partly accomplished through the "educational" segments of each autobiography, which include exhaustive definitions of autism, Diagnostic and Statistical Manual of Mental Disorders (DSM-IV) criteria lists, check-lists for determining ASD, and information and advice on a variety of related topics such as nutrition, exercise, special lenses, therapy, ways of engineering the environment, education, family life, dating, and work.

A strong motivation to inform and help others usually prompts the authors to reveal very personal information about themselves. Tammet explains in his opening chapter that "it is my hope that I can help other young people living with high-functioning autism" (12). There is an effort to share moments of shame as well as pride, moments of failure as well as success. They are willing to "tell it like it is" so that the reader can identify with them, and can see that it is possible to survive and also to thrive as a stranger in a strange land. Dr. Tony Attwood points this out in the Foreword to *Pretending to be Normal*: "The value of writing about her lifelong journey of exploration is that those with Asperger's Syndrome will recognize the same perceptions, thoughts and experiences. She is a fellow traveler. She offers genuine hope for the future" (Holliday Willey 9).

The authors in this study and many others like them seek to make the world a better place for people on the spectrum. They seek to inform the public and to enlighten us about the special gifts that individuals with autism offer to our society. As Liane Holliday Willey expressed: "I do not wish for a cure to Asperger's Syndrome. What I wish for is a cure for the common ill that pervades too many lives; the ill that makes people everywhere compare themselves to a normal that is measured in terms of perfect and absolute standards, most of which are impossible for anyone to reach" (10). When her dream comes true then she will have made the world a better place not just for people with autism spectrum disorder, but for the rest of us as well.

Works Cited

Bellis, Peter J. *No Mysteries Out of Ourselves: Identity and Textual Form in the Novels of Herman Melville.* Philadelphia: University of Pennsylvania Press, 1990.

Fitzgerald, Michael. *Autism and Creativity: Is There a Link Between Autism in Men and Exceptional Ability?* New York: Brunner-Routledge, 2004.

---. *The Genesis of Artistic Creativity: Asperger's Syndrome and the Arts.* London: Jessica Kingsley Publishers, 2005.

Grandin, Temple. *Emergence: Labeled Autistic.* New York: Warner Books, 1986.

Prince-Hughes, Dawn, ed. *Aquamarine Blue 5: Personal Stories of College Students with Autism.* Athens, Ohio: Ohio University Press, 2002.

Prince-Hughes, Dawn. *Songs of the Gorilla Nation: My Journey through Autism.* New York: Harmony Books, 2004.

Shelley, Mary. *Frankenstein.* New York: Penguin, 1983.

Tammet, Daniel. *Born on a Blue Day: Inside the Extraordinary Mind of an Autistic Savant.* New York: Free Press, 2006.

Willey, Liane Holliday. *Pretending to be Normal: Living with Asperger's Syndrome.* London: Jessica Kingsley Publishers, 1999.

Williams, Donna. *Nobody Nowhere: The Extraordinary Autobiography of an Autistic.* New York: Avon, 1992.

Further Reading

I. Autism and Writing

Bedrosian, J, et al. "Enhancing the Written Narrative Skills of an AAC Student with Autism: Evidence-based Research Issues." *Topics in Language Disorders* 23.4 (Oct 2003): 305–324.

Belmonte, Matthew K. "Human, but More So: What the Autistic Brain Tells Us about the Process of Narrative." Autism and Representation Conference Proceedings. Case Western Reserve University, Cleveland, Ohio. Oct 28–30, 2005. http://cwru.edu/affil/sce/Texts_2005/Autism%20and%20Representation%20Belmonte.htm.

Beversdorf, D, et al. "Network Model of Decreased Context Utilization in Autism Spectrum Disorder." *Journal of Autism & Developmental Disorders* 37.6 (Jul 2007): 1040–1048.

Blastland, Michael. "In Sickness and in Hope: A Conversation with Neil Vickers and Francesca Happé." *Prospect* Sep 2007: 1-3. http://prospect-magazine.co.uk/2007/09/insicknessandinhope.

Chew, Kristina. "Fractioned Idiom: Poetry and the Language of Autism." Autism and Representation Conference Proceedings. Case Western Reserve University, Cleveland, Ohio. Oct 28-30, 2005. http://cwru.edu/affil/sce/Texts_2005/Autism%20and%20Representation%20Chew.htm.

Davis, Megan, et al. Towards an Interactive System Facilitating Therapeutic Narrative Elicitation in Autism. University of Hertfordshire. http://homepages.feis.herts.ac.uk.

Fitzgerald, Michael. *Autism and Creativity: Is There a Link between Autism in Men and Exceptional Ability?* New York: Taylor and Francis, 2004.

---. *The Genesis of Artistic Creativity: Asperger's Syndrome and the Arts.* London: Jessica Kingsley Publishers, 2005.

---. *Unstoppable Brilliance: Irish Geniuses and Asperger's Syndrome.* Dublin: Liberties Press, 2006.

Fleche, Anne. "Echoing Autism." *The Drama Review* 41.3 (Fall 1997): 107–122. Literary Reference Center by EBSCO HOST. http://www.ebscohost.com.

Glastonbury, Marion. "Wild Work: On Picturing Ourselves and Others." *Changing English: Studies in Reading and Culture* 6.2 (Oct 1999): 135–144. Literary Reference Center by EBSCO HOST. http://www.ebscohost.com.

Greenwell, Bill. "The Curious Incident of Novels about Asperger's Syndrome." *Children's Literature in Education* 35.3 (Sep 2004): 271–284. Literary Reference Center by EBSCO HOST. http://www.ebscohost.com.

Heffner, Gary. "Echolalia and Autism." The Autism Home Page. http://sites.google.com/site/autismhome/Home/special-situations/echolalia.

Loukusa, S., et al. "Use of Context in Pragmatic Language Comprehension by Children with Asperger Syndrome or High-Functioning Autism." *Journal of Autism & Developmental Disorders* 37.6 (Jul 2007): 1049–1059. Literary Reference Center by EBSCO HOST. http://www.ebscohost.com.

Murray, Stuart. *Representing Autism: Culture, Narrative, Fascination*. Liverpool: Liverpool University Press, 2008.

Rimland, Bernard. Introduction to Donna Williams's *Nobody Nowhere*. New York: Avon, 1992.

Williams, Donna. *Autism and Sensing: The Unlost Instinct*. London: Jessica Kingsley Publishers, 1998.

--- *Exposure Anxiety: The Invisible Cage*. London: Jessica Kingsley Publishers, 2003.

Williams, Karen. University of Michigan Medical Center, Child and Adolescent Psychiatric Hospital. "Understanding the Student with Asperger's Syndrome." Online Asperger's Syndrome Information and Support site (OASIS). http://www.udel.edu/bkirby/asperger/karen_williams_guidelines.html.

Zunshine, Lisa. "Theory of Mind and Experimental Representations of Fictional Consciousness." *Narrative* 11.3 (Oct 2003): 270-292. Literary Reference Center by EBSCO HOST. http://www.ebscohost.com.

II. Related Literary Works (selected list)

Andersen, Hans Christian

The Complete Fairy Tales and Stories. Garden City, New York: Doubleday, 1974.

The Diaries of Hans Christian Andersen. Selected and translated by Patricia L. Conroy and Sven H. Rossel. Seattle: University of Washington Press, 1990.

The Fairy Tale of My Life [autobiography]. New York: Cooper Square Press, 2000.

Hans Christian Andersen's Visits to Charles Dickens, as Described in his Letters. Copenhagen: Levin and Munksgaard, 1937.

Only a Fiddler: A Danish Romance [novel]. New York: Hurd and Houghton, 1871.

In Spain [travel]. London: R. Bentley, 1864.

The Stories of Hans Christian Andersen: A New Translation from the Danish. Translated by Diana Crone Frank and Jeffrey Frank. Durham: Duke University Press, 2005.

The Story of My Life [autobiography]. New York: Hurd and Houghton, 1871.

The True Story of My Life [autobiography]. 1847. http://www.onlineliterature.com/hans_christian_andersen.

The Two Baronesses: A Romance [novel]. New York: Hurd and Houghton, 1869.

Anderson, Sherwood

Dark Laughter [novel]. New York: Liveright Publishers, 1960.

Kit Brandon [novel]. New York: Scribner's, 1937.

Many Marriages [novel]. New York: B. W. Huebsch, 1923.

Marching Men [novel]. New York: John Lane Company, 1917.

Poor White [autobiographical novel]. New York: New Directions, 1993.

Selected Letters. Knoxville: University of Tennessee Press, 1984.

The Sherwood Anderson Diaries, 1936–1941. Athens, Georgia: University of Georgia Press, 1989.

Sherwood Anderson's Memoirs. Ed. Ray Lewis White. Chapel Hill: University of North Carolina Press, 1969.

Sherwood Anderson's Secret Love Letters. Baton Rouge: Louisiana State University Press, 1991.

Short Stories. New York: Hill and Wang, 1962.

A Story Teller's Story [autobiography]. Ed. Ray Lewis White. Cleveland: Case Western Reserve University, 1968.

Tar: A Midwest Childhood [autobiography]. Cleveland: Case Western Reserve University, 1969.

Windy McPherson's Son [novel]. Chicago: University of Chicago Press, 1965.

Winesburg, Ohio [short stories]. New York: Random House, The Modern Library Edition, 1947.

Carroll, Lewis (Charles Lutwidge Dodson)

Alice's Adventures in Wonderland and Through the Looking-Glass. Oxford: Oxford University Press, 1971. All quotations taken from this edition.

The Diaries of Lewis Carroll. Ed. Roger Lancelyn Green. New York: Oxford University Press, 1954.

Eight or Nine Wise Words about Letter Writing. Oxford: Emberlin and Son, 1911.

The Humorous Verse of Lewis Carroll. New York: Dover, 1960.

The Hunting of the Snark. New York: Lewis Carroll Society of North America, 1992.

The Letters of Lewis Carroll. Ed. Martin Cohen. New York: Oxford University Press, 1979.

Lewis Carroll's Diaries: The Private Journals of Charles Lutwidge Dodgson. Five Volumes. Luton: Lewis Carroll Society, 1993–2007.

Nonsense Verse. London: Edward Hulton, 1959.

The Pamphlets of Lewis Carroll. Charlottesville: University Press of Virginia, 1993.

The Story of Sylvie and Bruno. London: Macmillan, 1980.

Symbolic Logic. New York: C. N. Potter, 1977.

Dickinson, Emily

Emily Dickinson's Herbarium: A Facsimile [not poetry—a fabulous reproduction of the "herbarium" into which Emily pasted plants and flower specimens and carefully labeled them]. Cambridge, Massachusetts: Harvard University Press, 1996.

The Master Letters of Emily Dickinson. Amherst, Massachusetts: Amherst College Press, 1986.

Open Me Carefully: Emily Dickinson's Intimate Letters to Susan Huntington Dickinson. Ed. Ellen Louise Hart and Martha Nell Smith. Ashfield, Massachusetts: Paris Press, 1998.

The Poems of Emily Dickinson. Ed. R. W. Franklin. Cambridge: Harvard University Press, 1969.

Selected Poems and Letters of Emily Dickinson. Ed. Robert Linscott. New York: Doubleday Anchor Books, 1959.

Grandin, Temple

Animals in Translation: Using the Mysteries of Autism to Decode Animal Behavior. New York: Scribner's, 1995.

Animals Make Us Human: Creating the Best Life for Animals. New York: Houghton Mifflin, 2009.

Emergence: Labeled Autistic [autobiography]. New York: Warner Books, 1986.

Thinking in Pictures: My Life with Autism [autobiography]. New York: Vintage, 2006.

The Way I See It: A Personal Look at Autism and Asperger's. Arlington: Future Horizons Publishers, 2008.

Melville, Herman

Bartleby the Scrivener: A Story of Wall Street. Hoboken: Melville House Publishing, 2004.

Billy Budd, Sailor, and Selected Tales. Oxford: Oxford University Press, 1997.

Collected Poems. Alexandria: Chadwyck-Healey Inc., 1996.

The Confidence Man. Normal: Dalkey Archive Press, 2007.

Correspondence. Evanston: Northwestern University Press, 1995.

Journals. Evanston: Northwestern University Press, 1989.

Moby Dick. New York: Pearson Longman, 2007.

Redburn: His First Voyage: Being the Sailor-Boy Confessions and Reminiscences of the Son of a Gentleman. New York: Modern Library, 2002.

Typee, Omoo, Mardi. New York: Penguin Putnam Inc., 1982.

White-Jacket: The World in a Man-of-War. Charlottesville: Univeristy of Virginia Press, 2000.

Prince-Hughes, Dawn

Aquamarine Blue 5: Personal Stories of College Students with Autism. Athens, Ohio: Ohio University Press, 2002.

Gorillas Among Us: A Primate Ethnographer's Book of Days. Tucson: University of Arizona Press, 2001.

Songs of the Gorilla Nation: My Journey through Autism. New York: Harmony Books, 2004.

Tammet, Daniel

Born on a Blue Day: Inside the Extraordinary Mind of an Autistic Savant: A Memoir. New York: Free Press, 2006.

Thoreau, Henry David

Collected Poems. Alexandria: Chadwyck-Healey, 1996.

The Essays of Henry D. Thoreau. New York: North Point Press, 2002.

In Wilderness is the Preservation of the World. New York: Sierra Club, 1967.

Journal. Princeton: Princeton University Press, 1981.

Letters to Various Persons. Boston: Ticknor and Fields, 1865. http://www.archive.org/stream/lettersvarpersons.

The Maine Woods. Princeton: Princeton University Press, 2004.

Thoreau's Comments on the Art of Writing. Lanham: University Press of America, 1987.

Walden and On the Duty of Civil Disobedience. New York: Collier Books, 1962.

A Week on the Concord and Merrimack Rivers. Princeton: Princeton University Press, 2004.

Wild Fruits: Thoreau's Rediscovered Last Manuscript. New York: Norton, 2000.

Whiteley, Opal

The Fairyland Around Us. [Opal self-published this book, and copies are rare, but a copy of it can be found online] http://www.efn.org/%7Ecaruso/fairyland/canvas-preface-03.htm.

Opal Whiteley Manuscript Collection [a delightful gathering of her college notebooks, diaries, and personal papers] at Knight Library, University of Oregon.

The Singing Creek Where the Willows Grow: The Mystical Nature Diary of Opal Whiteley. Ed. Benjamin Hoff. New York: Penguin, 1986.

Willey, Liane Holliday

Asperger Syndrome in Adolescence: Living with the Ups, the Downs, and Things in Between. London: Jessica Kingsley Publishers, 2003.

Asperger Syndrome in the Family: Redefining Normal. London: Jessica Kingsley Publishers, 2001.

Pretending to Be Normal: Living with Asperger's Syndrome [autobiography]. London: Jessica Kingsley Publishers, 1999.

Williams, Donna

Autism and Sensing: The Unlost Instinct. London: Jessica Kingsley Publishers, 1998.

Everyday Heaven: Journeys Beyond the Stereotypes of Autism [autobiography]. London: Jessica Kingsley Publishers, 2004.

Exposure Anxiety—The Invisible Cage: An Exploration of Self-Protection Responses in the Autism Spectrum and Beyond. London: Jessica Kingsley Publishers, 2003.

Like Colour to the Blind: Soul Searching and Soul Finding [autobiography]. London: Jessica Kingsley Publishers, 2001.

Nobody Nowhere: The Extraordinary Autobiography of an Autistic. New York: Avon, 1992.

Somebody Somewhere: Breaking Free from the World of Autism [autobiography]. New York: Times Book, 1994.

Yeats, William Butler

Autobiographies. New York: Scribner, 1999.

The Autobiography of William Butler Yeats. New York: Collier, 1965.

The Collected Letters of W. B. Yeats. Oxford: Oxford University Press, 1986.

Early Essays. New York: Scribner, 2007.

The Gonne-Yeats Letters: Always Your Friend. London: Hutchinson, 1992.

The Irish Dramatic Movement. New York: Scribner, 2003.

Later Essays. New York: Scribners, 1994.

Memoirs. New York: Macmillan, 1972.

Mythologies. New York: Macmillan, 2005.

The Plays. New York: Scribner, 2001.

Yeats's Poems. Ed. Norman A. Jeffares. Dublin: Gill and Macmillan, 1989.

Lightning Source UK Ltd.
Milton Keynes UK
19 June 2010

155815UK00002B/6/P